Mariah Wolfe & Charlotte Lindhardt

Narcissistic Men
10 Strategies to Deal With Toxic Husbands, Fathers, Boyfriends, and Co-Workers

Mariah Wolfe
2020

Narcissistic Men
10 Strategies to Deal With Toxic Husbands, Fathers, Boyfriends, and
Co-Workers

Authors: Mariah Wolfe & Charlotte Lindhardt ©2020
Translation: Charlotte Lindhardt
Editor: Jill White
Published by: Psychotherapist Mariah Wolfe
www.visiblehearts.com

Artwork: Jesus Pulido.
http://jesuspulidoart.wixsite.com/port

Printed by Amazon ©2020 1st edition

Typseset by Crystal Peake Type

Narcissistic Men
10 Strategies to Deal With Toxic Husbands, Fathers, Boyfriends, and Co-Workers

Contents

Dear Reader   7

About Mariah og Charlotte – the authors   11

Narcissism – Facts About The Disorder   13

The Background For The Narcissist Diagnosis   16

The Official Symptoms Of Narcissism   18

Which Kind Of Narcissist Is Your Narcissist?   21

The 3 Diagnoses   23

Questions About Narcissism   24

Narcissists In Movies   35

How Does The Narcissistic Man Get Into Your Life?   37

The Consequences Of Being Close To A Narcissist   42

Traumatic Bonding – Why It Is So Difficult To Leave A Narcissist   51

Addicted To Drama   56

The Narcissistic Wound   58

The Methods Of The Narcissist   61

Flying Monkeys – When Even Your Closest Relations Don't Understand   92

Consequences Of Long Term Relationships With A Narcissist   100

Emotional Incest   113

How Do I Live With A Narcissist?   125

Co-Parenting With A Narcissist   134

The Narcissist In The Workplace And In The System   146

How Do You Free Yourself From A Narcissist?   151

After The Narcissist   157

In A New Relationship – Now What?   162

Conclusion   165

Read more   169

Dear Reader

A FEW WORDS FOR YOU BY MARIAH WOLFE

This book is written on the basis of my extensive knowledge and numerous questions, which occur when talking about narcissists. I have asked questions myself. I have received questions from my clients; from the media during interviews; and from people contacting me through e-mails and letters. The questions are both the most common, classic ones, and those which until now have remained unanswered in literature.

The book is written in first-person based on Mariah Wolfe's expertise and knowledge about narcissism. It has a solid foundation in my work with relatives to narcissists during the last 20 years – and last, but not least it is the result of my own experience as a daughter of a narcissistic father and my personal work of letting go of the consequences of this upbringing; as well as the result of my friend and co-writer Charlotte Lindhardt's experience with a narcissistic mother.

Our aim is to give you the answers, you need in order to move on and reclaim your life after being in contact with a narcissistic wife. Finally, the book addresses your possibilities as a relative, when you are unable to do what is most expedient: Entirely breaking off the contact.

The book has a chapter about being a child of narcissistic parents, so you can help your children in the best way possible. No matter whether you are family, friend, partner, or colleague, we recommend reading the ENTIRE book. There may be an angle useful for you in one of those chapters which at first glance seem irrelevant for your situation.

Narcissists are different because people are, and there are no clear answers to everything. Therefore, reading the entire book – even if some parts seem irrelevant – will expand your knowledge and understanding of your own situation. Knowledge is power, and the more knowledge you acquire, the better for you.

The book supplements personal therapy and offers a new point of view on your experiences.

The narcissist destroys your confidence in yourself and in other people. It is difficult regaining that trust and confidence and therefore you can supplement the knowledge from this book with workshops and therapy conversations. At connect@visibleharts.com you can contact me for online conversations about having a relationship to a narcissist and/or moving on from one.

Publicly, the narcissist can seem charming, engaging, giving, generous, and funny. Often, this person radiates warmth and love, which makes everybody like him.

Everybody wants to befriend this person; wants to be close to the person. However, those who ARE closely connected with the narcissist, see another picture. Those people are subjected to manipulation, demeaning, ridicule, fury, lies, and brainwashing.

There used to be a huge number of narcissists in public business, the media landscape, and high-prestige jobs. Today, there are many more people with narcissistic characteristics everywhere in society – or maybe, we have become better at spotting them. Nevertheless, we find relatives and colleagues to narcissists everywhere in all branches of trade, and in all social strata.
Narcissists are siblings, mothers, fathers, and partners - men and women in all ages and all social classes. Therefore, no matter where you meet them it might be good for you to know something about what you need to pay attention to.

This book gives you an insight into the narcissists and the mechanisms of their behavior. It suggests what you can do before, during, and after your encounter with the narcissist; and how you can take care of yourself.

Besides concrete knowledge about the narcissists and their behavioral patterns, there are plenty of cases from the real world.

Throughout the book, I have put in statements, which briefly and precisely nails it, when it comes to the specific narcissistic conduct.

When reading this book, you might recognize situations and feelings; and you may want to write down your thoughts. I suggest that you buy a small notebook, and after each chapter you can make a note of what made the biggest impression on you. When writing, what affected or helped you, it sticks better in your memory.

If you are connected to or have been close to a narcissist, you can experience some emotional reactions, when reading the book – anger, sorrow, shock. Therefore, make sure that you can get peace and comfort from others and yourself during this process.

It may take a long time to come to terms with the after- effects caused by a narcissist, but with this book you have taken a step forward because the tools and our experiences can help you. Remember, that you always can go back to the book and your notes. That way, you will find out how far you have come in your healing process.

There are a lot of examples in this book. When reading them, please remember that similar examples can be found in most relations with narcissists – whether it is in the workplace, in families, in friendships, or in relationships.

This book begins with facts about narcissism.

What are the official symptoms? What causes it? Which consequences does it have, when you are close to a narcissist? Then follow chapters about the methods of the narcissists, and how you may experience this.

Besides, I discuss the consequences of living with a narcissist, and what you can do, if you must relate to a narcissist in your day-to-day life. Lastly, you will get some tools as to how you liberate yourself from the narcissists, and how to repair the after-effects.

Finally, we send a huge thank you to the readers of the first draft of this book, and to the proofreaders of the English version. Your help was indispensable.

Thank you for being here and taking yourself seriously. Thank you for allowing this book to lead you a step in the right direction.

If you want to be sure to have the skills to spot the narcissistic abuser, now and in the future, feel free to jump on my FREE mini course here: https://bit.ly/nomorenarc

Warm regards, Mariah
NB. Feel free to connect with me on Facebook: https://www.facebook.com/BeingMariah/

**DISCUSSING WITH A NARCISSIST
IS JUST LIKE GETTING ARRESTED:
ANYTHING YOU SAY OR DO,
CAN AND WILL BE USED AGAINST YOU.**

About Mariah og Charlotte – the authors

Mariah Wolfe hit the media spotlight in 2011, when her narcissistic father, the Danish actor Poul Glargaard, took his own life and blamed her for it. Mariah decided to step forward and tell publicly about what it was like growing up in a world of manipulation, lies and violence. That created a platform, from which she tirelessly has informed and educated clients and others about narcissists, and the consequences of getting into the clutches of them.

Today, Mariah travels the world, and she holds sessions and conversations with her clients via video calls and WhatsApp. Her books and online courses help thousands of people through difficult experiences. Learn more at www.visiblehearts.com.

Charlotte Lindhardt is the oldest child in a – seen from the outside – typical family with mother, father, and three daughters. She grew up with her mother's fits of rage and silent treatments, which the entire family adapted to. In 1996, when Charlotte was 23, it came to a permanent break with her parents, who didn't want to accept her choice of education, boyfriend, or friends. Her parents disinherited her, and today they claim that they have only two daughters. Therefore, Charlotte has experience with life as a grown-up "orphaned" child of narcissists.

Charlotte has a MA in history and semiotics. She lives in Herning in Jutland, Denmark, and works as a freelancer. Learn more at www. konsulentcl.dk and www.ubirex.dk.

Narcissism – Facts About The Disorder

Before I describe the symptoms and explain them, let me emphasize that the word "narcissist" no longer is used as a term of abuse about self-absorbed people. Those who are taking a lot of selfies, talking endlessly about themselves, or following their dreams, are NOT necessarily narcissistic. The core of the narcissistic disorder is *that they use other people and promote their own interests at the expense of others*.

This is not: "No, I don't bother cleaning the house; do it yourself," or that you get hurt because another person doesn't want to do the same as you. If that was the case, 50 % of us would be narcissists – and of course it isn't so. Narcissism is a serious diagnosis - a mental disorder.

It is possible to have narcissistic traits without being a narcissist. Humans don't fit into boxes. There is a difference between being narcissistic and a narcissist.

If a person has narcissistic traits, he is within therapeutic reach and can be helped. However, this requires that the person recognizes his responsibility for his actions. Like everything else in life, the prerequisite for change is to acknowledge those of our actions that do not work for us or downright hurt others. We can't recognize that on behalf of others; only the person himself can realize that something is wrong, and then act on it. Actually, the narcissist is not important. Here, you and your feelings are the main issue.

Before we get to that, let us summarize what the premises for narcissists and persons with narcissistic traits are.

When we know what we are dealing with, we can be inspired to act upon it and build hope.

#EXAMPLE

Anita has been in a relationship with Allan for three years. She has lost contact with friends and family, who gradually began seeing the change within Anita, and who told her what they observed. When she told Allan about it, he claimed that her family and friends didn't understand her and that they didn't act in her best interests.

Slowly, Anita withdrew herself from others. Allan supported her when she did so. Her friends tried to get her out of the relationship, but as they began realizing that she didn't budge, they gave up and let her go.

Anita is on sick leave from work. Every day, she fights an internal and external battle. The internal battle is about her and Allan's relationship. She doesn't feel good when she is with Allan, but he has clearly stated that this is her own fault – and she believes him. She has almost managed to mute the little voice deep inside her heart, which tells her that Allan isn't good for her. The external battle stands between her and the man, who made her feel more loved than ever before.

It takes nothing to invoke his fury. One wrong word, a blouse in the wrong color, or bad news on TV, and he is furious. He yells and screams, until his spit stands still in the air. Sometimes for almost an hour. He just keeps going – on and on. She has tried everything. Asked him to stop. Explained that she feels he is overreacting. Tried giving him a perspective. Appealed to his common sense. Walked over and tried to hug him. Laughed it away. Nothing works.

When Allan gets furious, his eyes go black, and he is out of reach. She can't walk out on him, either. Then he grabs her and shakes her, blames her and says that she doesn't love him.

So, she just listens. Meanwhile, the words etch her heart and soul. They eat her up. They devour her joy. Her energy. It is like an omnipotent poison seeping from his words and through her skin into her body, mind, and heart. She will never get out of that relationship. That's what it feels like. Whenever she tries, she is pulled back in with promises about change, kind words, and sex. Again, and again. She is in such a desperate need for loving words and peace of mind that she lets him do it, even though she deep in her heart knows that after a week, everything will be the same.

NOT ALL THAT GLITTERS IS GOLD
- AND THE NARCISSIST'S AFFECTION
IS NOT LOVE EVEN THOUGH
IT MIMICS IT

The Background For The Narcissist Diagnosis

THE MYTH - MISUNDERSTOOD SELF-LOVE

Narcissus was a young man renowned for his beauty. His parents were the river god Cephissus and the nymph Liriope. Narcissus was proud and despised those who loved him. In order to prove their devotion toward his magnificent beauty, some of his admirers even committed suicide.

The goddess of revenge and justice, Nemesis, saw this and lured Narcissus toward a lake, where he discovered his own reflection in the water. He fell deeply in love with what he saw, without realizing that it was his own mirrored face.

He was unable to draw himself away from the image in the water because he had developed an untouchable love, which never could be requited. Narcissus lost the will to live and withered away. From his remains grew a narcissus flower – a lily.

The story has a wonderful symbolism. Narcissus was unable to love because he already was in love.

Not with himself, but with the image of himself. Therefore, he was incapable of loving others. His love for the image in the water could never be fulfilled because he destroyed it, as soon as he reached for it. You will know that, if you have ever seen your own reflection in water and put your hand down through it.

Apart from giving the narcissistic disorder its name, the myth also explains what it is like being a relative, friend or partner.

Those loving a narcissist "obliterate" themselves in order to prove their love to him or her. That is the essence of being close to a narcissist.

You MUST annihilate yourself, your needs, rights, wishes, and dreams, when proving your love – and proving it is a must. The narcissist will demand it from you.

IF THE NARCISSIST LOSES CONTROL OVER YOU, HE WILL TRY TO CONTROL HOW OTHERS SEE YOU.

The Official Symptoms Of Narcissism

According to the American diagnosis, there are 9 official symptoms of narcissism.

The narcissist ...

1. feels grandiose and important. He seriously feels that he is better than other people – and acts accordingly;

2. has no close relations. He might say that this is the case, but this is not true. At closer look, the relations are superficial, and they are treated in a way, so they constantly deliver the narcissistic supply,

3. doesn't think that your friends and your family are good enough – and they are a threat toward him monopoly on you! Your friends and family won't do. The narcissist will tell you that they don't understand you, don't support you, and that they envy you. If the narcissist, in exceptional cases, thinks that someone in your life is good enough, he will charm the person and turn that person against you,

4. uses a lot of sarcasm and can be extremely patronizing. If you confront him with that behavior, it will be dismissed with "I'm just joking," or a surprised reaction that "you don't understand what I really mean!"

5. expects special treatment from everyone because he feels extraordinary and better than other people,

6. manipulates, lies, and exploits others – with a smile. Sometimes, he even manages to make it sound funny and charming, when he does so,

7. gets furious over trivial matters and thinks that others are responsible for fixing it,

8. is convinced that if someone dislikes him, it is out of pure jealousy,

9. will, in the beginning, take you along on a joyride of positive statements, praise, and sweet-talking of your special bond, and will make you feel fantastic – but as time goes by, you will gradually feel inferior, often without realizing how and when it happened.

If your partner, boss, friend or others fulfill AT LEAST 5 of these criteria, there is a large risk that this person is a narcissist. Hurry up, pack, and run far, far away.

If you have come close to a narcissist, you may get the feeling that there is something wrong with you, when your sense of reality is in disharmony with the one the narcissist presents you with.

Maybe you can't put words to it, but you have the feeling that something is not quite right. When you realize, what is wrong, it is time for you to act – and this process is all about you.

Narcissists have a special ability to paint a picture of themselves as the victims, where other people feel sorry for them. It is never the narcissists' fault, when things go wrong with jobs, relations, etc.
Problems are always caused by the outside world and other peoples' lack of understanding, support, and/or goodwill.

That is, you can't change that person, save that person, love the narcissist enough, talk sensibly with the narcissist, or make the narcissist join therapy

– and if it finally happens, the narcissist might charm the therapist into thinking that the narcissist is right. Then the narcissist will throw it in your face and tell you that you are the one with a problem.

However, YOU might benefit from therapy, if you are or have been close to a narcissist. It can be very difficult to understand how another human being can behave so absurdly, as narcissists tend to do.

Therapy provides you with tools and support for you to take care of yourself against the narcissist. It will free you and confirm that what you see and think about it is true. It enables you to see the experience more clearly and from new angles.

Do remember to ask the therapist or the psychologist, whether he or she is familiar with narcissism and treatment of the after-effects. Often, I have had clients, who told me that they were talked down to by therapists who didn't realize the seriousness of this topic.

A certain sign that a person is a narcissist, is the illogical denial of everything, which the person does. A narcissist can explain any bad behavior away by blaming others – and especially you.

For example, a narcissist will tell you: "If you hadn't done what you did, I wouldn't have had to treat you badly."

THE NARCISSIST IS YOUR WORST ENEMY BUT WILL:
- ARRIVE DISGUISED AS A HERO.
- DARKNESS DISGUISED AS LIGHT.
- HATRED DISGUISED AS LOVE.
- PREDATOR DISGUISED AS A FRIEND.
- LIE DISGUISED AS TRUTH.
- BETRAYAL DISGUISED AS LOYALTY.
- INDIFFERENCE DISGUISED AS EMPATHY.
- ASSAILANT DISGUISED AS A LOVER.

Which Kind Of Narcissist Is Your Narcissist?

In the latter years, the world's biggest media – the Internet – has come up with types like "the martyr narcissist", "the depressive narcissist", and "the introvert narcissist". Sometimes, my clients describe their relatives as one of these three.

The martyr narcissist is supposedly someone, who always plays the victim – over and over. Often, he will say things like: "After everything I have done for you, this is how you repay me!" However, narcissists generally use guilt as a weapon, and often it is the trademark of a classic narcissist to play the victim card. Even so, not all martyrs are narcissists.

The depressive narcissist lies in the darkness and seems down and depressive: "Everybody thinks that I am lazy. I am just the black sheep of my family.
I might as well give up!" The idea behind this strategy is that you, being a relative/family member, is supposed to reply: "Oh no, you are not! I find you clever and smart, and you should never give up!"

In that way, you provide the narcissist with his supply. You spend your energy on him, and often the worst episodes take place, when you are going to do something which is good for you or which you have been looking forward to. Then you have to cancel, for naturally you are not that self-absorbed that you will walk away from the poor couch potato.

However, you will quickly realize that this person is acting – and may not be aware of it himself, but again, you can't blame him for doing it because: What kind of monster would accuse a poor, depressive person for faking it?!

The introvert narcissist is supposed to be especially sensitive, empathy-lacking and restrained. This person talks less and is not as prominent in the landscape, and when the introverted type finally opens up, it is often with condemning and critical statements.

This type is passive aggressive and will often say things like: "Yes, we will do whatever you want to do. As usual." Or: "No, don't even think about me. I am not important."

However, the fact is that if the person, whom you call a narcissist, doesn't have at least 5 out of the 9 classic criteria, he isn't a narcissist. It may be a deeply self- absorbed, empathy-lacking person behaving like a martyr or being introvert.

If you think that one of these three popular descriptions fit a person who causes you problems, you are free to call that person whatever you like.

Sometimes it is helpful when we can set things to words to describe the issue.

No matter which type of narcissist you have met, and no matter which diagnoses or popular descriptions he fitted, the most important thing is that you learn to take care of yourself.

ASK YOURSELF THIS:
WHO DO YOU BECOME,
BECAUSE THE PERSON IS LIKE THIS?
WHO DO YOU BECOME,
WHEN THE PERSON BEHAVES NARCISSISTICALLY?
WHAT DO YOU NEED,
IN ORDER TO FEEL GOOD IN YOUR OWN LIFE RIGHT NOW?

The 3 Diagnoses

Narcissism belongs in the category of "dyssocial personality disorder". This category contains sociopathy, narcissism, and psychopathy. There is a lot they have in common, but there are distinctions.

In short, the differences are:

The psychopath differs from the narcissist by being completely indifferent to other peoples' thoughts. She is cold as ice and calculating – and he stands by it. The narcissist thinks that he is a good person, while the psychopath knows that he is a predator – and proud of it. A good example is the crime series **Luther** with Ruth Wilson playing the role of an ice- cold, calculating psychopath toying with the police.

The sociopath doesn't have an inner core or "self", and will change looks and personality like a chameleon, when he meets someone who triggers his envy. Sociopaths want to become other people, and when they meet a person they admire, they will try to imitate the person in any way. A really good movie about this topic is **The Hand That Rocks the Cradle** with Jamie Lee Curtis.

Since people and diagnoses not are static and predictable objects, you might experience that the narcissist displays character traits from the other personality disorders.

It might be the colleague, who imitates you in the workplace because you are doing a good job, or a partner, who fluctuates between maintaining that he wants the best for others, while he at the same time boasts his ability to be calculating and manipulative.

Questions About Narcissism

WHAT PERCENTAGE OF A POPULATION ARE NARCISSISTS?

It is impossible to answer, since all of us are born with the sound, narcissistic traits, which we need in order to survive. Only a minority develops a definite personality disorder. The number of people with a "pure" diagnosis is minimal, but many have narcissistic traits, and naturally, it is impossible to count those people. Therefore, it doesn't make sense to give an estimate.

However, I would like to try, based on Danish statistics. In Denmark, 70% of all families are affected by abuse of addiction in one way or another. Since many addicts carry narcissistic traits, it is probably about half of them, i.e. about 35 % of the population, which have unsound behavioral patterns and share some narcissistic traits, for instance irresponsibility and lack of empathy - whether there is an addiction or not. This means that there are just as many "co-dependents". They fail to take care of themselves, but circle about others like small satellites, and they blame others for their own feeling of being a victim. These people choose to become invisible and give way for others on behalf of their own health and joy.

It is impossible to be close to a narcissistic person without being somehow affected. What all those affected relatives have in common is that they somehow shut down for themselves. Emotionally, energetically, socially – or all. They shut down to protect themselves, to not be invaded or feel unwelcome, but that is unavoidable.

ARE NARCISSISTS MOSTLY MEN OR WOMEN?

Based on the answer regarding the number of narcissists in society, it is equally difficult to answer this question about the distribution of narcissists between the genders. My experience is that I meet most men with classic narcissistic traits, and most women with depressive and/or martyr traits. Even though we can't estimate the number between the genders, some traits are typical for a gender.

Human beings are not robots, and therefore there are so many variables and uncertainties that it is impossible to say "this is how it is" for certain.

Why do people become narcissists – are they born with it?
When it comes to infants, there are two important circumstances:

1. They are omnipotent.

2. They are boundless.

The word omnipotent origins from:
Omni = everything. Potent = influential, strong. The child is (mostly) alone inside its mother's womb and is fed via the umbilical cord. The entire universe exists for the child's purpose, and the universe IS the child. The child has nobody to reflect, to copy. It has no consciousness of not being the universe, or of other peoples' existence in the world. The child is omnipotent – and that is how it is supposed to be. The infant shall not – neither in its mother's womb nor as a newborn – have to relate to others. It just has to get its needs fulfilled. To feel that it influences everything.

The omnipotence is gradually removed, layer by layer, when the infant doesn't get all its needs covered; when it reflects in other peoples' eyes; when it interacts with smile, laughter, and the scent, sound and touch of other human beings. We don't have to think about it or do something actively for this process to happen. In its essence, the infant's sound and natural development will do it. However, if the small child is deprived of contact with others; if the child gets ignored and is deprived of contact, warmth, intimacy, smiles, and eyes, to mirror itself; then the child fails to develop true and close connections with other people.

This is why it is horrendous, when parents spend more time looking at their cellphones than being in contact with their child – and when they let their child spend too much time with an iPad or another kind of screen.

That is not contact – and contact is one of the most important foundations for the development of children. Even when the mother or the father walks the baby in the baby carriage, the baby can feel whether there is genuine contact or not; and the baby feels abandoned, when the primary adult seems out of reach. All of us are capable of feeling whether others are mentally present or not. You are, I am – we are born with it, but it can be shut down.

When an infant is deprived of contact, it is unable to create the neural connections which enable us to acknowledge our feelings and to feel connected with others. Without feelings and intimacy, there is created a basis for psychopathy or narcissism.

Infants are boundless, without boundaries, and the experts explain it thus: The infant is unaware of it having a physical delimitation. As a newborn, it doesn't know that it is a separate human being from its mother, father, or other people around it. The infant fails to understand that the parents can have their own needs, and it gets frustrated and unhappy, when it doesn't feel connected, or when its needs are unfulfilled.

During the first three months of its life, the child will experience a gradual toning down of precisely these two things: omnipotence and boundaries.

The child will realize that it is not omnipotent: "I don't get everything, I need. Other people are not at my free disposal. Sometimes I have to wait for food. Sometimes I am cold and will not get warm straight away. Sometimes I need my mother to touch me, and she is not there straight away." All of this is a part of the child's sound and natural development, as the mother is unable to be there 24 hours a day; even though she has to be there as much as possible.

The unpleasant experiences from a child's first months are a part of shaping how the child will feel within itself and with others for the rest of its life. If these experiences are presented in a good way; i.e. the mother is available most of the time; it will not be unpleasant. The child will not feel deserted, but gradually learn that it isn't omnipotent, and it will develop in a sound and natural way. For instance, if the child is hungry, it reaches for its mother's breast, but she isn't ready. She has to remove her bra, and maybe the child whimpers a bit, before the mother can feed it. This is a good way to learn that you can't get everything you want, straight away.

It is NOT damaging for a child to immediately get what it wants. There are several cultures, where the mother doesn't leave the child at all during its first year, and in these cultures, the people seem to possess a very high degree of empathy and feeling of solidarity.

Bali is a good example of this. The Balinese have an unwritten consensus that during the first year, the child is always so close to its mother that it can feel her skin and the warmth from her body. These children trust that their needs are covered, and they grow up reassured that the world will be good to them – and therefore they are easily capable of being good toward others.

In the Western culture it is not always possible to be in close proximity of our children for a whole year – but all mothers do their best, and that's how it is supposed to be. However, if it takes too long, before the child is breastfed, the child will lie alone getting a feeling of "I am worthless, and I don't get what I want, and my needs are not fulfilled." Maybe the mother and the father don't have the proper reserves, and they hit or shake the infant. Then the child will feel worthless.

Very few parents hurt their child on purpose. However, no parents are perfect, and sometimes the circumstances in an otherwise sound family make it possible for a child to develop narcissism. Children are different too, and some are more vulnerable and need more intimacy than others. The lack of intimacy can starve a child emotionally, without the parents being aware of it.

The father – and other people close to the child – can have a tremendous significance for the child. If the mother, or the primary caretaker, is absent, it is possible for other adults to influence the child, so it grows up as a strong and sound person. Intimacy, contact, and respect can do a lot in order to give the small child a good start in life.

The boundlessness disappears gradually after the birth. The child learns that "mother isn't me, and I am not mother, and there is a difference between me and everything else outside me." The lack of boundaries is a good thing, but we must learn that I have boundaries, as well as you do. It must happen in a way for the child to experience a sound process of separation. If that isn't the case, it is possible to develop a personality disorder.

It would be interesting, if we were able to find out what specifically happened to my father – if we were able to make a movie, which showed his childhood, what his mother did, what exactly made him narcissistic. My grandmother has told me about her first experiences as a mother – that she felt it as a personal insult, when my father as a newborn baby screamed and cried. Probably, my grandmother was a victim of the times with the general assertion that "screaming develops the lungs".

My grandmother saw a baby as a status symbol; something she could show as a prize won in a contest. The way I knew her, she was not a person who understood love or intimacy. She, too, was a victim of her own upbringing, and she didn't live in an age, where that was a natural thing to take care of – she wouldn't even have known where to look for the proper tools to help herself.

The characteristic of a narcissist is the lack of self-worth. Where other people have a jar, which is more or less full or empty, the narcissist's self-worth jar is always empty – and it has a hole in the bottom. Every time, he tries to fill the jar, or when others try, the content runs out the other end.

Therefore, the narcissist needs an endless supply of validation and acknowledgment from others because the narcissist is incapable of acknowledging and loving himself from the inside.

The narcissist can't feel his own inner worth, unless others tell him about it. However, he IS able to tell himself that he is the most important person in the whole world, that he is better than others – and that is not a worthy value, that is a disease.

Regrettably, it is also a condition which makes it difficult for the narcissist to see himself relating to others and understanding that his behavior is inappropriate. Narcissists do not feel their low self- worth, and their conduct of feeling more worthy than others is an unconscious strategy in order not to sense the feeling of being worthless.

Of course, you may feel sorry for them – as long as it doesn't influence how much you give of yourself. It is a classic trap to believe that compassion and boundlessness can help them. When we are close to people, who are going through a hard time, most of us find it easy to give up ourselves, our boundaries and our needs in order to make way for the other person and that person's needs. The problem is, that narcissists will NEVER get better, and they will never leave any space for you in that relation.

Narcissism is, as you can read, not a congenital condition, but a disorder developed from the environment in which the child is brought up. Often, the basis of narcissism is founded during the first months of its life. However, narcissistic behavior can also occur later in life, if a person has been subjected to something during the upbringing.

For example, many adult children of alcoholics display either an exaggerated form of co- dependency, or the opposite: lack of understanding and empathy, as well as an excessive self- centeredness. These traits can easily be confused with narcissistic characteristics. This is the consequences of a childhood, where the person didn't have room enough to sense himself or his needs, and therefore he develops a kind of numbness so that he can survive, and the numbness follows him into adulthood.

But often, adult children of addicts are, in some way or another, still in touch with the pain inside them because their parents actually tried to be there for them during the first months of their lives, and therefore the parents managed to create a foundation of intimacy and security. Therefore, adult children of addicts often are capable of seeking therapy and doing something about the feeling of numbness.

The narcissists' lacking the ability of feeling themselves often began that early, that they lack this foundation, and therefore they do not recognize the pain as their own. Narcissism is not physically hereditary, but to a high extent emotionally hereditary.

CAN YOU DEVELOP NARCISSISM FROM A CHILDHOOD WITH TOO MUCH ATTENTION?

No! But! If there is no respect for the boundaries of the small child, the result may be the same, as if the child lacks intimacy and contact. A part of the sound contact is that the adult senses and respects it, when the child has had enough, and lets the child have a break. Excessive contact without respecting the boundaries is not a good kind of contact.

Anyone, who has been close to an infant, knows how the child can turn its head away, close the eyes, or in another way set boundaries for itself in relation to its surroundings. If the parents fail to understand that, they signal to the child, that this family disrespects boundaries, and the child may become apathetic or whining. Sometimes you experience that children "zoom out", when
they have become used to not being allowed to set boundaries. They get a faraway look in their eyes, and they are out of reach. All children can become engulfed by something and forget time and place – that is not the same, as when a child "zooms out".

To indulge – to yield for an inclination or desire is a wonderful expression, which is often misinterpreted. Indulging with material things is not love.

Food is not love. Even though a lot of people comfort themselves with food and use things to replace love and intimacy. They do not do it out of evil, but because they don't understand how to embrace and feed another human being (or themselves) emotionally.

We just have to be there. Look others into their eyes with love. Hold them. Listen to them. Encourage them to talk about the things inside them. That is very difficult in a culture, where material items to such a high extent have taken over and turned human beings into slaves, and where most people feel inadequate.

THE SEA DOESN'T TEACH YOU HOW TO SWIM. YOU DO.
THE SEA ONLY PROVIDES YOU WITH THE WATER TO SWIM IN.
SO DOES THE NARCISSIST. HIS BEHAVIOR DOESN'T TEACH
YOU HOW TO SET BOUNDARIES AND TRUST YOURSELF.
YOU DO. THE NARCISSIST ONLY GIVES YOU A LOT OF
BULLSHIT FOR PRACTICE.

CAN FIGHTING IN A WAR TURN YOU INTO A NARCISSIST?

No, but you can develop temporary narcissistic or psychopathic characteristics because war calls for our deepest survival instincts. We will do anything to stay alive. When you have been in a survival mode for a very long time, and maybe even have had to take the lives of others, you can become emotionally cold because your experiences have been too difficult for your mind to contain and handle.

Therefore, at times veterans can seem empathy-lacking and cold. They have had to protect themselves to such a high extent that they may have had to shut down their personality. The war, the blood, and the fear live inside them, and if that is not continuously taken care of, they can develop PTSD – post-traumatic stress disorder – which is extremely difficult to overcome in a society, where intimacy and love not are remedies used for medicine, in the public sphere. We tend to hand out a pill and 10 x 45 minutes of sessions with a distant professional, and that rarely helps.

Evidently, very traumatic experiences like war or growing up without space for being oneself can't be fixed with 10 hours of talking. It takes more than that.

CAN A NARCISSIST BECOME A STALKER?

Stalking is when a person follows you, spies on you and lets you know that it happens, so it creates a sense of insecurity. Not all stalkers are narcissistic, and not all narcissists become stalkers, but it is very common that narcissists stalk their relatives, if they set up boundaries after having left the narcissist.

The reason for this behavior is that the narcissist – not consciously, but subconsciously – feels that he owns the relative, and that the relative "owes" something to the narcissist. If the relative is incapable of seeing that the narcissist becomes insistent, will show up at a possible new address, make phone calls, write, follow the relative on social media, and push the limits to extremes. The narcissist will neither hear nor read the boundaries, which you set, and he will continue trying to get a foot in the door, until you either give up or let him inside, or you just stop answering the attempts of contact.

Narcissists will also sometimes ask you to define what it will take for you to let them back into your life. However, even though you clearly are able to tell them what it takes – respect, communication, compassion, and intimacy – it will never happen. Even so, they will promise all of the above, and they will believe in it themselves.

A common characteristic for all narcissists is that they disrespect your boundaries. They will continue pushing them, crossing them, and ridiculing them. Make them insignificant. Wrong. They may even say that they are going to change their behavior, and that they will begin to respect your boundaries. It just doesn't last. Maybe for a short while, and then they are back to the old patterns.

Remember that narcissists lie. They lie to themselves. To others. To you. And they believe in their own lies, that's why they are so good at "selling the goods". A skilled salesman believes in his own product. You may doubt whether you are wrong, hear wrong, interpret or remember something wrongly, when they pursue you. Narcissists use as an excuse that they just want to take care of you, that they worry about you, or that they are simply being considerate. Since they believe in it themselves, they might be able to persuade you into accepting this sick kind of conduct – you will doubt whether you are being fair or whether your boundaries are too rigid.

You know, you have every right to set up these boundaries, even though others – narcissists or not – think that they are unfair. Don't hold back on contacting the police and associations for stalkers' victims in order to get the support you need, so you can feel safe and well in your own life.

CAN YOU BECOME ILL FROM BEING CLOSE TO A NARCISSIST?
It is almost impossible NOT to become ill, if you through a longer period have been close to a narcissist. The narcissists manipulation teaches you to suppress your own needs and feelings – and this means that you probably ignore your body's signals when you need peace, breaks, rest, and mental space. This may lead to severe stress and depression.

When we are constantly tense, larger amounts of cortisol are released, and that is not healthy for our body. It affects our absorption of nutrition, and it affects our lymphatic system. Therefore, it makes good sense that those who have been close to a narcissist for a long time get seriously ill. As adults it is pointless to blame the narcissist. Instead we must remove ourselves from the things that make us ill and take good care of ourselves.

Today we know that a lot of adult children of narcissists struggle with eating disorders and hormonal diseases and that makes sense in a sad way - since children of narcissists are not nourished emotionally, their bodily nourishment system malfunctions.

WHEN YOU TRY TO EXCUSE
THE BEHAVIOR OF THE NARCISSIST,
DON'T LOOK AT WHAT HE SAYS,
BUT AT HIS CONCRETE ACTIONS.
HOW DOES IT HELP, I
F HE SAYS THAT HE WILL STOP LYING
AND START LISTENING TO YOU,
IF HE DOESN'T DO IT?

Narcissists In Movies

The literature and the big screen have several excellent descriptions of narcissists and their behavior.

The novel **The Picture of Dorian Gray** by Oscar Wilde is from 1890 but is easily read and still universally valid. The novel describes the narcissist's love for himself, and it has been filmed several times.

The handsome, young Dorian Gray is painted for a portrait. He is convinced that life's only virtue is beauty and youth, and therefore he makes a wish for the painting to age instead of himself. His wish comes true, and Dorian Gray maintains his good looks but becomes evil and selfish – and the portrait turns into a hideous monster.

The movie **Gaslight** from 1944 builds on a play by Patrick Hamilton from 1938. A young woman (Ingrid Bergman) meets a man, and they marry after a two-week whirlwind romance. He persuades her into giving up her career as an opera singer, and she abandons her friends and moves to London with him.

The husband is a classic narcissist with an overwhelming love in the beginning; then isolation of the chosen one – combined with manipulation and fits of rage, almost driving the woman to insanity.

Drop Dead Fred is a quirky little movie from 1991 featuring Rik Mayall and Phoebe Cates. She plays Elizabeth, who is oppressed by her dominant and narcissistic mother – right until Elizabeth's invisible childhood friend, the crazy Drop Dead Fred, turns up and makes her revolt. Despite its serious topic, the movie is a black comedy with plenty of humor and madness.

A more recent example is the Leonardi DiCaprio- movie **The Wolf of Wall Street** from 2014. It is based on real events and describes the rise and fall of Jordan Belfort, who became a wealthy stockbroker by lying, cheating and manipulating his way up.

Two examples of female narcissists in movies are **Notes on a Scandal** from 2006 where Judi Drench plays the British teacher who takes advantage of a younger colleague with no guilt or remorse - and **Osage County** from 2013 where Meryl Streep plays the severely dysfunctional and narcissist matriarch.

How Does The Narcissistic Man Get Into Your Life?

You may be born into a family with a narcissist; you may enter a workplace with a narcissistic person; there may be one among your acquaintances; or you may fall for a narcissistic person. Unfortunately, there are many ways in which you can encounter one. What happens, really, when you fall for a narcissistic husband or boyfriend?

The narcissists are always on the lookout for new "supply", i.e. people who will give them attention, no matter if that attention is positive or negative. A narcissistic person feels most alive when interacting with others. In superficial relations, they can mirror all the deliciousness, which they see in others, as something they hold themselves.

For instance, narcissistic persons always fall for people, who contain whichever qualities they want themselves, and they will create an alliance with you; making you believe that they hold exactly the same qualities as you do, or that their own qualities fit perfectly with yours. In other words: The narcissist will mirror himself in you, so you feel important and amazing.

The narcissist might say things like: "You are so unique. Your sensitivity and your huge compassion for others make you extra vulnerable. I am just the same, and people like us must take care of one another." Or: "You are so strong and so much in control of your life. It is rare to meet a kindred spirit, who is as wise as you are."

Observe that these statements emphasize the two of you as someone who both possess the same characteristics, and therefore you have something special in common. Of course, the narcissist possesses them – otherwise he or he couldn't recognize them within you – but they are not activated. They will never show in daily life, which you will find after having been some time together on Cloud Nine. The characteristics are hidden beneath an extremely low self-worth, and they are rarely in use – only to gain power or other advantages in the relationship with others.

The narcissist dreams of the one true love, and he is truly capable of putting on a show and "love bomb" you with words, caresses, adventures, money, gifts, sex, or whatever the narcissist senses that you need, in order to lure you into their spider's web.

You will feel that no one has ever loved you so intensely or truly before. You have never been seen and understood so beautifully and sensibly, as the narcissist does. That is hard to resist, and if you are deceived and caught in his web, it doesn't mean that you are less intelligent or more naïve than others. We all want to feel loved, to feel special and important, and that is what the narcissist gives you. For a short while – and that is the problem. It is nothing but hot air, and it doesn't last.

The narcissist will be busy trying to commit you with children, money, duties, important job functions, marriage, buying a house, or anything else which makes it hard for you to turn your back on him and walk away.

All relationships – or most of them, at least – begin in the seventh heaven as something special, until everyday life begins, the gilt cracks and reveals that this is not just a fixer-upper, but an unfixable ruin of a human being, who doesn't accept neither sense nor sensibility. However, in the beginning you will become the prince or princess, who is the center of all fairytales. It doesn't last. Over and over you will experience the cycle with which the narcissist slowly destroys you. It is on infinite repeat.

Love bombing begins with idealization. Then follows devaluation, and then rejection. At first, you will be regarded as the most fantastic creature, which the universe has ever encountered. Then, you will be torn to pieces and humiliated, and lastly, you will be rejected and deemed useless.

Since you don't understand that this is a sick pattern, it may be difficult to see through it, and that's why you are going to react like everybody else: You will try fixing it. You will take responsibility, and your thoughts will run in circles trying to find a solution.

You will do everything in your power to make him happy - and you will fail.

"If I just do this and that, then we will find our way back to love and the unique essence of our relationship" – and this attitude gives the narcissist precisely what he wants: attention and power. The cycle will repeat itself, and the "love", which you long for, becomes a lesser and lesser part of your relationship, while the devaluation of you grows, until you are convinced that you are the one, who broke and trashed the love, and that you are a bad and unlovable person.

This, however, doesn't mean that you shall keep from falling in love, or that you have to be on guard toward people, who see and value your good qualities.

What you must do, is have a strong relationship with yourself, thus enabling you to feel that you are "enough" without another person's acceptance, approval, or need for you. Then you are free to walk away, as soon as it becomes unpleasant, and your boundaries are disrespected. You will become more difficult to manipulate and brainwashed into believing that you owe someone something or that you must live up to certain expectations.

Ask yourself: "If I wasn't trying to fix things and make him happy all the time, would he want me?" If the answer is no, then you are merely a facilitator and your relationship is fake, hard as it is to realize.

WHY DO YOU THINK THAT YOU WERE THE ONE FALLING FOR THE
SUPERFICIAL CHARM OF THE NARCISSIST AND GOT TREATED BADLY?

    BECAUSE I AM TOO QUIET? NO.
    BECAUSE I TAKE UP TOO MUCH SPACE? NO.
    BECAUSE I AM A BAD HUMAN BEING? NO.
    BECAUSE I AM STUPID? NO.
    BECAUSE I AM ANNOYING? NO.
    BECAUSE I DESERVED IT? NO.
    BECAUSE I PROVOKED HIM? NO.
    BECAUSE I AM EASILY FOOLED? NO.
    BECAUSE I DON'T FUNCTION WITH OTHERS? NO.
    BECAUSE I ALLOWED IT? NO.
    BECAUSE I AM A LOSER? NO.
    BECAUSE I ATTRACTED IT? NO.
    BECAUSE I AM TOO NAÏVE? NO.
    BECAUSE I AM DIFFERENT FROM OTHERS? NO.
    BECAUSE I AM A PLEASER? NO.
    BECAUSE I BELIEVED THE LIES? NO.
    BECAUSE I AM TOO DELICATE? NO.
    BECAUSE I WAS TOO OPEN? NO.
    BECAUSE I WAS TOO TRUSTING? NO.
    BECAUSE I IGNORED THE WARNING SIGNALS? NO.
    BECAUSE A NARCISSIST SIMPLY JUST ABUSES AND MISUSES
        OTHERS? YES.

The Consequences Of
Being Close To A Narcissist

The thing which you are not allowed to see until you get really close to a narcissist is the narcissistic fury, which is a rage completely out of proportions with the actual problem and which can seem overwhelming and terrifying. Until then, you might even have felt honored at being the chosen one – wow – you were worthy enough to spend time with this amazing person. Hold the thought, for that is exactly what the narcissist wants you to feel.

Most likely, you ARE fantastic. The narcissist rounds up people, who possess the characteristics, which he wished he had himself – and he will try to make you believe that you are equals. But slowly and unconsciously, the narcissist begins to feel inferior, and that is unbearable to him. Instead of working with himself, he will begin putting you down. Making you feel wrong and less worthy.

So, when you experience the narcissistic rage for the first time, it feels overwhelming and unexpected.

However, since you still feel deeply loved, you are going to write it off as a one-off thing, and you forgive it. However, it is never just a one-off. It is going to happen again and again and again … and you will be blamed. EVERY TIME.

Your boundaries will be moved, your self-worth will be broken down, and your common sense will effectively be eliminated through the narcissist's changes between: "You are amazing, I'm sorry that I get angry, I hope you'll understand," and "You make me so furious, you let me down, you don't give me what I want, you owe me, and you are not doing this properly."

AS SANDPAPER WEARS THE WOOD,
THE NARCISSIST'S CLEVER CHANGES BETWEEN SUGARY
AND MEAN SLOWLY LOWERS YOUR STANDARDS,
AND IN THE END YOU THINK
THAT THE MEDIOCRE OR THE NEUTRAL IS AMAZING
- IT WILL BE ENOUGH FOR YOU THAT HE ISN'T MEAN OR
FURIOUS.
YOU WILL END UP BELIEVING THAT LOVE IS WHEN HE IS NOT
HURTING YOU
- INSTEAD OF EXPECTING TRULY LOVING ACTIONS.

Words ARE magic because we believe in things, if we hear them often enough. Our brain is wired that way. In Antiquity and far up in the Medieval Age, people believed that Earth was flat, and that our planet was the center of the universe. Now science has proven that Earth is round and part of an infinite universe with other planets and galaxies. In the same way, the narcissist makes us believe that he is the most important thing in the whole world – until we discover that out there, there is another truth.

To a lesser scale, the narcissist uses the same methods. He tells you over and over that you are inadequate, full of errors, unloving, and the narcissist blames you for the lunatic behavior – and sadly, subconsciously that makes sense to many people, since our culture is filled with people with low self-worth and self-esteem, and people don't believe in themselves.

The narcissist believes that he is the center of the universe, and he makes us believe that it is our own fault that he behaves badly. The narcissist expects you to deliver the narcissistic supply, i.e. making him feel good, comfortable, loved, and recognized. These feelings were the ones you fell for, and the ones he was so good at giving you in the beginning.

Usually, it takes longer and longer between you getting that lovely present, while the narcissist's expectations for you to deliver it rises. If you don't, you may be subjected to the rages, which often is out of proportion compared to the actual problem, and where the only purpose is making you feel unworthy and that you "owe" something. That keeps you in the relationship because, as the narcissist says: "Now, where I have given you everything." or "After everything I have done for you." In other words, you owe him something.

NARCISSISTS LOVE MAKING OTHERS FEEL INFERIOR, MENTAL, UNWORTHY, WEIRD, UNLOVABLE, WRONG AND CRAZY BECAUSE THEY DEEP DOWN FEEL LIKE THAT THEMSELVES. BY MAKING OTHERS FEEL THAT WAY, THEY FEEL SUPERIOR.

When narcissists are unable to receive the positive feelings and the caring recognition from their surroundings, they happily accept the negative ones. Therefore, there are many narcissists with psychopathic characteristics in the prisons and among criminals.

Any attention feeds the narcissists ego, and that is one of the reasons why anger and arguments fail to improve his behavior.

Many women and men get their self-worth ruined by a narcissistic partner, parent, or superior.

Anyone can become subjected to narcissists, since they at first glance seem more than sound.

Therefore, there is no reason to blame yourself, if you fall for one. Just hurry away, if you find out that it is someone close to you.

The narcissist loves giving you the cold shoulder - for shorter or longer periods – and then you become like a small satellite, which fearfully and hopefully floats around and constantly keeps an eye on him. After all, you have – without noticing it – learned that he is the center of the world. Your focus is moved from yourself to him, more and more, since you never know him state of mind. Even though this is not physical violence, it can trigger emotional or complex PTSD, called C-PTSD.

C-PTSD means that these things take up more and more space in your life:

- Shock and denial

- Lacking confidence of your perception of the world

- Confusion and concentration difficulties

- Anger, frustration, mood swings

- Anxiety and fear

- Guilt, shame, and self-criticism

- You isolate yourself from others

- Feelings of sadness and/or hopelessness

- Lack of joie de vivre

- Feelings of being put outside the rest of the world, in a bubble, or feeling numb

- Strong reactions to even the little things like a car door slamming, or other unpredictable sounds.

#EXAMPLE

Charlotte's mother, Inge, is narcissistic with a depressive and martyr-like behavior. There is always something indefinable wrong with her; something which "the doctors are too arrogant to figure out", and the entire family is pushed around according to her mood. Sentences like "Don't you feel ashamed about this?" and "What do you think the neighbors will say, when you do X?" have been mantras for Charlotte's entire childhood. When Inge couldn't get it the way that she wanted, by shouting at or accusing others, she walked out and said that now neither her husband nor her children knew, when she would return.

When Charlotte became a teenager and started having opinions of her own, her mother would punish her with silence for days at the time. If Charlotte said something, it would be ignored, even though it was a "good morning" or "hello". Charlotte's father, Ebbe, and her sisters were all instructed in following the mother's directions.

Once Charlotte bought a scarf for her grandmother for Christmas, and Inge got furious, since "this is not what your grandmother needs!" Inge didn't speak to her daughter for 10 days because Charlotte refused to swap the scarf, which she had paid for herself.

For years, Charlotte reacted with strong sentiments of guilt and shame. It didn't take much for her to feel guilty over things that she didn't do, should have done differently, or ought to have done for others.

Charlotte spent many sleepless nights speculating how she could become a better person.

When Charlotte turned 18, she moved out from her parents' home as quickly as possible. Her mother's attempts to manipulate her, and so did the monstrous rage followed by periods with freezing silence, and aged 23 Charlotte had to put a hold on the relationship.

That was caused by her parents demanding that she should break up with her boyfriend because they didn't like him.

A few years later, Charlotte learned that her parents had started telling other people that they had two children (not three), and she received a letter from a lawyer notifying her that her parents had written a will and disinherited Charlotte. Her parents used a paragraph, which you normally use toward mentally handicapped – something which Charlotte describes as a ritual honor killing: They couldn't kill her for real, but they could write her out of the family history.

To the narcissist, it is easier to pretend that a problem or a person doesn't exist, when it confronts the narcissist's scheme of things and self-perception. This goes for both families, in relationships, and work colleagues.

THE NARCISSIST CAN BECOME INFURIATED OVER SOMETHING, WHICH YOU PERCEIVE AS A SMALL THING, AND GO TOTALLY BERSERK WHEN YOU POINT IT OUT. YOU HAVE ABSOLUTELY NO RIGHT TO HAVE AN OPINION!

Narcissists are experts in putting on a façade. They appear empathic, friendly, kind, understanding, fun, generous, humble, attentive and accommodating toward others - just as you saw him in the beginning - but behind closed doors they perform the most horrendous violations toward the ones closest to them.

The narcissist can fool anyone: collaborators, business associates, lawyers, professors, and managing directors. Even specialists like psychiatrists, psychologists, and psychotherapists might be fooled, if they are unaware of what to look for. It doesn't help you, when the authority, who was supposed to support you in your perception of reality, also gets dazzled by the narcissist.

You start feeling desperate, but instead of thinking: "I have to find the courage to get away and rediscover my inner strength," you start thinking: "I have to convince him to treat me properly. Make him realize that he doesn't have to be an asshole, when I only want to do what is best for him." In other words, you begin to take responsibility for the narcissist and him behavior instead of taking responsibility for you and what is best for you.

When you have been entangled by a narcissist, you will feel – maybe for the first time in your life – that you have met someone who sees you, who hears you, and who understands you. Consequently, you let your guard down and yield to love or friendship.

Since you may never have experienced such an intense "love" before, you don't know which warning signals to look for, and you ignore the small weird or unpleasant episodes. You become an expert in forgiving, and your boundaries move without you noticing, and gradually you will put up with more and more things.

The narcissist's behavior is illogical, and therefore you may find that your reactions become illogical too. You begin to manipulate or try to, you start yelling, and you get furious because your opinions and needs get ignored, and you become a victim for others to save. This happens because you have given up on yourself.

#EXAMPLE

Dani's story:

"I started shouting just like him. Personally, I will NEVER forget this, and I was in shock that I could react like this. Deep down I knew that he was yelling and screaming about something that was way out.

But, by all means, I just wanted him to shut up and stop twisting and turning my words. I wanted him to understand what the endless lies, his deception, his yelling and screaming did to me.

This gave me the feeling of being soooo far from who I am and ever have been. I saw myself trying to catch his words and twist them just to make him understand what he did to me. Afterwards, it seems totally surreal that I didn't even think about ME getting away from him, but only about making HIM understand and take responsibility for his behavior."

You can forget everything about:

- getting any of the events to make sense

- getting the narcissist to understand what he has done

- making the narcissist realize that any of what happened, or a choice he made during the situation, was wrong

- getting the narcissist to understand you and/or your feelings

- getting an excuse from the narcissist

- expecting positive changes for the future.

That is, unless the narcissist finds that a confession will benefit him in the situation.

The narcissist is resistant to facts. You may offer endless proof and documentation, but the narcissist will still dismiss them or explain them away – or simply call you touchy or empathy-lacking. Only when it benefits him – for instance in order to shorten a punishment for a criminal action – a narcissist will admit the deeds and say sorry.

**YOU WILL NEVER GET A NARCISSIST TO ADMIT THAT HE IS A VILLAIN,
BUT THE NARCISSIST WILL GLADLY
TAKE ON THE ROLE AS A HERO OR A VICTIM.**

As opposed to narcissists, the psychopaths will lie as easily as they breathe, and they will stand by doing it because they feel that they have the right to get what they want. Narcissists also lie easily but they don't admit it because they believe in their own lies. Their compass of truth is turned upside-down, and they are so good at telling lies that they believe in them. For instance: "I had to break the traffic rules in order to make the traffic flow. It was a matter of safety!"

When you are close to a narcissist, you really have your work cut out for you. Everything you have learned about sound communication and relations will be tested – and fail in the narcissist's world

The narcissist makes it hard for you to relax and feel safe, and you will begin being constantly on guard and in defense mode. You will spend endless amounts of energy guessing how to say something or how to behave in order to stop the narcissist from getting furious.

You will be drained to a degree which others can't imagine, unless they have been there themselves, and you might end up getting anxiety, depression, and suicidal thoughts.

NARCISSISTS GLADLY USE MONEY IN ORDER TO MAKE YOU DEPENDENT ON THEM.
THEY LEND YOU MONEY, PROMISE YOU MONEY, OR PAY FOR SOMETHING EXPENSIVE, SO YOU "OWE" THEM - AND THEY WILL USE THIS TO GET UNDER YOUR SKIN!

Traumatic Bonding – Why It Is So Difficult To Leave A Narcissist

Our brain is wonderful!

Back in the ages, when we lived in tribes, it was extremely important that the tribe could stick together no matter what happened in hard times. The tribe's culture, moral code, and values often were premises for surviving war, famine, and illness – or at least to get through in order to rebuild life.

Therefore, our brain is pre-programmed to adapt and to be quick to forget tremendous pain. It longs for pleasantness and will strive for it at any cost.

The brain is able to forget violations, or to tone down the violence of it, or to explain it away in order to "make you stay in the tribe". In the old days, it was necessary for the individual to put up with a certain degree of unsound behavior and stay with the tribe, otherwise you wouldn't survive.

Besides that, we are programmed to bond with people with whom we have experienced something hard. Think about your own life and the people close to you. You have probably been through hard times together with many of them, and that has created a special bond between you. War, famine, and illness tie us together. That is called traumatic bonding.

That is clever when we are a part of a sound community, but it is terrible when we are close to a narcissist – no matter whether it is a family member or a partner. The traumatic bonding means that we tend to tie ourselves closer to the narcissist, when he violates us and afterwards feeds us a bread crumb of something which looks like love or acceptance.

Your bond with the narcissist is fake. It has nothing to do with love. It is simply a sign that your brain behaves like it would do, if your tribe was in war or struck with a plague epidemic. In other words: You are sound enough, but this is not the right place to be, when you are close to a narcissist.

To make the traumatic bonding happen faster, the narcissist may pull you out of your normal social surroundings and cut you off from your network. The narcissist will soon tell you that the people, who question your relationship with the narcissist, either privately or in the workplace, don't get you, don't want what's best for you, and simply envy you because of the person you are or what you have achieved.

The narcissist will say things like: "Yes, of course you are free to do what you want, but I don't understand why you want people in your life, who don't support you, when you are happy. Do they really want you to stay single? I don't get it – you and I have something unique, and apparently they don't like that."

Maybe you will defend your friends/family/work colleagues, but the narcissist will insist, shrug, and say: "That's up to you. I would never put up with it. I don't want people like that around me."

In that way, the narcissist makes himself a role model and judges you as being incapable of securing yourself the best life possible. Very few of us like that, and that makes you act irrationally. You wonder whether the narcissist is right, and what you can do about it.

He may also play on your loyalty and say things like: "Oh, I really thought that what you and I had was something magical and precious, but you just walk about and tell the whole world that it is crap? I see that I really misjudged you."

The narcissist threatens to dethrone you from the pedestal which he placed you on in the beginning; to make the two of you incompatible, so you lose the relationship, and he makes it seem wrong to confide in others, when something feels hard.

Slowly, but securely, the narcissist isolates you, so there is no one to talk to, confide in, or get support from. This means that you have no one, who can validate your experience of reality. In the end, the only "truth" comes from the narcissist.

The long-term effect of this phenomenon causes your personality to wither away, and it is replaced with a new personality which suits the narcissist's behavioral pattern.

You might have heard about people who got kidnapped, and after a certain time as prisoners actually preferred to stay in the relationship with their jailer because this new relationship makes it safer to stay where you are. This effect is called The Stockholm Syndrome. The term comes from a robbery in Stockholm in 1973, where innocent people were kept hostage for five days, and even during the trial they were reluctant to expose the robbers.

#EXAMPLE

Jay and Marge have been married for 30 years. After five years abroad, they have moved back home, and they join family therapy because their children are mentally and physically ill. Marge tells me that "it is due to mood swings, psychic violence and emotional blackmail". Jay blames Marge for causing it because she is indulgent, weak, doesn't set boundaries, and gives the children too much money and too many things.

In therapy, Marge is unable to give examples of what she accuses Jay of doing, and she agrees with him that he has been a strong role model and a great father, and she says that she is the one with the problem because she is too weak.

When I get her in a one-to-one session, she pours out examples of GROSS mental abuse, humiliations, and manipulation from Jay. It turns out that this is a chaotic home, where everybody always takes Jay's mood into consideration. Marge's eyes get distant when she tells me about it – it is like watching a flood of words, just pouring out in an endless stream, without her being conscious about it.

I try to repeat for Marge what she just told me, and I try to get her to confirm that Jay is doing all these things – to confirm everything she has just told me, but as soon as she has to be mentally present and consciously confirm her experiences, she refuses to do it. Then she maintains that she is the problem.

When I talk to Jay alone, face-to-face, he spends the entire session telling me how amazing he is, and he tries to make me agree with him. He doesn't want to talk about his behavior toward the children. That is a minor issue. He is far more important. He refuses to talk about the family and reasons that I - on my blog - wrote an article concluding that "happy parents make happy children" – and it is far more important that he is happy in order to be a good father for his children.

The children also join me for individual sessions, but they have been equipped with a recorder and told to record the conversation for Jay to listen to afterwards. He says that this is just because he needs to better understand what to change. Naturally, the children tell me nothing about their father's behavior.

Three months later, the family – i.e. Jay – chooses to move to Dubai. I receive an e-mail about it, and it is embellished with pompous statements about how amazing I am as a therapist, and how helpful their "therapy course" (a total of six sessions including the individual conversations) with me was.

Addicted To Drama

When you feel anger, sorrow, love, fear, or desire, the feeling is inside you. Maybe something outside you provokes it, but the reaction is inside you.

When something is inside you, it is yours. That is awesome, since this means that you have the means to change it.

You can't change things outside you, but you can change yourself. Your way of reacting. Your emotions. This means that even though a person outside you behaves in an offensive way, it is YOUR responsibility how you feel about it and react.

Reactions are natural. Of course, you get fearful, angry and unhappy, if, for instance, you have been violated. That is your right and a natural cause from it. The same things happen when we are being pushed over by the narcissist. It is natural to react, get angry, shout, cry, or feel fear. But it is – and that is the thing which may seem provoking – your choice.

The narcissists LOVE IT when they can make you react. Your reactions are their supply, their energy, and they nourish their feeling of being alive – and they can justify themselves through your reaction. They create so much drama around themselves, and they know EXACTLY which buttons to push in order to provoke a reaction within you.

When you choose not to react, not to show emotions, not to let panic or fear take over as a reaction to the narcissist's drama; then the narcissist will increase the drama – or become cold as ice and shut you out.

When you are shut out or put in a situation, where there is no drama, but silence and emptiness, then you might experience that you long for being together with the narcissist – EVEN THOUGH you know that the narcissist is the troublemaker and the one pushing you around. In that way, you will feel that you miss the drama – at least that gave you a connection.

WHEN THE NARCISSIST SAYS THAT HE HAS CHANGED, I TRUST HIM - JUST AS MUCH AS I TRUST SERIAL KILLERS, SCORPIONS, POISONOUS SNAKES, AND SHARKS SMELLING BLOOD.

#EXAMPLE

Charlotte's mother was effective at coaxing Charlotte to open up and feel close and confidential with her. It was not until Charlotte became a teenager and developed her own opinions that her mother started punishing her with silence.

It could last for days, and during that time Charlotte felt very lonely within the family. Even though the punishment was caused by something where Charlotte was certain that she was right, she sometimes succumbed just in order to reestablish the contact with her mother and the rest of the family.

The pattern was always the same:

Charlotte asked her mother whether they could talk about it. Then her mother would deny that there was anything to talk about at all. Then Charlotte asked her again. Then followed a huge row, which also might involve Charlotte's father – on her mother's side, naturally. When the row was over, and Charlotte had apologized, her mother would again act overwhelmingly friendly. She would once again let Charlotte come back into the family community, and the entire family would act as if nothing had happened.

The Narcissistic Wound

The narcissist is extremely vulnerable – even though he will never admit it, but rather will manipulate you into believing that YOU are vulnerable. Vulnerability is not a bad thing, but it feels like it when it is exploited.

A narcissist will perceive every tiny sentence as critique, turn it against you and use it to make you feel guilty.

For instance, if you ask someone you are dating: "How was work yesterday? I tried calling you." Maybe you asked out of pure interest, but the narcissist is not going to see it as such, but as criticism.

The narcissist hears every spoken word through a filter, which turns what actually was said into a kind of criticism. "All right, now he is cross because I didn't answer the telephone. He thinks that I am obliged to answer, whenever he calls. I have to be available even though he KNOWS that I was busy at work."

This provokes a reaction within the narcissist. This reaction is completely disproportionate with reality, and it stems from the huge, bottomless pit of lack of love, which resides inside the narcissist. You can never intellectually or emotionally explain the narcissist that you meant something else – or teach him to understand the good intention behind something. Narcissists have an open wound which always distorts messages into being AGAINST them, and that is what they react upon.

This is called "the narcissistic wound" and explains why narcissists fail to react or why they don't perceive the world like other people do. The reason is that they are unable to learn it, since that wound can never heal. And that is so painful to live with that they – unconsciously – will do anything not to feel it.

The narcissist's behavior doesn't make sense, and it will most likely drive you insane, if you try to make sense out of it or try to understand what happens.

The narcissist feels lesser worth than others, and unfortunately most of us have a tendency – because of an inbred who-do-you-think-you-are-attitude within our culture – to make ourselves smaller than we really are. We are afraid to unfold our whole and true potential, to show that we can shine and be strong, goal-oriented and committed because we fear getting told that we are too much, take up too much mental space, that we feel better than others, and that we are self-absorbed and dominating.

Naturally, no one is worth more than others – and no one is worth less than others. This is just a false myth which we carry along.

However, since we think that it is true, we often make us smaller than we are in order to fit in.

Particularly in love relations, where we make ourselves smaller in order not to make the other person feel small. That is completely wrong. The larger and more beautiful we show ourselves to the world, the more others can choose to become inspired by us – just look at Dalai Lama, the coach Tony Robbins and all the movie stars and musicians in the world. They inspire us, and no one tells them to turn down for their beautiful personality.

The same goes for you. You shall not diminish yourself in order to fit with a partner with a low self-worth. That is not your responsibility – neither is fixing that. Your partner has to find his own motivation and do the work on his own in order to stand in his own light.

The poem on the next page phrases it beautifully – I hope that it makes sense to you, no matter whether you believe in a god, an energy, or you are an atheist. In the poem, you can replace religion with something which makes sense to you – for instance, the universe.

OUR DEEPEST FEAR BY MARIANNE WILLIAMSON

Our deepest fear is not that we are inadequate.
Our deepest fear is that we are powerful beyond measure.
It is our light, not our darkness That most frightens us.

We ask ourselves
Who am I to be brilliant, gorgeous, talented, fabulous?
Actually, who are you not to be?
You are a child of God.

Your playing small Does not serve the world.
There's nothing enlightened about shrinking
So that other people won't feel insecure around you.

We are all meant to shine, As children do.
We were born to make manifest The glory of God that is
within us.

It's not just in some of us; It's in everyone.

And as we let our own light shine,
We unconsciously give other people permission to do the same.
As we're liberated from our own fear, Our presence
automatically liberates others.

The Methods Of The Narcissist

Can you communicate on a grown-up level with a 5-year-old? Lead a constructive dialogue with reflection and structure?

No. The narcissist is emotionally just as mature as a 5-year-old, so stop believing that you can lead an equal, adult dialogue. Just like a child can throw itself on the floor in the supermarket and kick with legs and arms, while screaming, the narcissist may react childishly when he doesn't get it the way he wants it. There is no difference – and just as the child in the supermarket may be out of pedagogic reach, so is the narcissist.

At first glance, it would be easier just to hold your fire, since it would be a waste of time and energy to try to reach a narcissist. However, we can't avoid bumping into narcissists during a whole lifetime, and therefore it could be helpful to have some tools to see through their methods.

Narcissistic personalities have an arsenal of various methods at their disposal, when they need to manipulate and control their world, or when they need attention. One thing, which never ceases to surprise and send shivers through the participants on my online groups and workshops, is how typical these methods are – almost everybody recognizes the methods. It becomes evident that the narcissist in no way can or is able to see that he uses a certain method in order to achieve something.

This chapter is about the most typical methods. Along the way, you can try finding examples of when your narcissist used these methods, and you can try to describe how that made YOU feel, and which type of person YOU become, when you experience these methods. Do they work on you? How?

TRIANGULATION
– WHEN THE NARCISSIST USES OTHERS AS A WEAPON

Triangulation is a recognized and well-known narcissistic technique, where the narcissist uses arguments, which aren't his own, against you. In that way he gains two things. Firstly, he stumps you because you are unable to defend yourself or discuss it properly with him, since "he didn't say it". Secondly, he drives a wedge between you and the person, who allegedly said what he uses as an argument – because it may very well be a lie.

"The other day, I told my friend about our argument because I thought that he could help me see what was going on. He said something that really made me think. He mentioned that sometimes mental illnesses are hereditary. Has anyone in your family ever been admitted to such a hospital?"

You can't defend yourself against this poorly hidden hint that you could be mentally ill. If you try, he will simply say: "Why do you get so aggravated about it? I didn't say it. I would never dream of calling you mentally ill. What is wrong with you, since you get so easily agitated? I simply don't understand it. I wish that I could help you."

Again, he will more than insinuate that there is something wrong with you, that he doesn't understand you, and that he disclaims any responsibility.

If you were able to record what he said and explain to him, what he was doing, he would say something like: "Why are you attacking me like that? You misunderstand everything I say. I feel like I can't say anything without you getting angry. Apparently, I have to attend a class in communication in order to be your partner. Things HAVE to be said YOUR way, otherwise you get aggressive and furious.

Have you ever considered that this is something, you have to work on?" – and thus, the dialogue will continue, and he will never, at any time, take responsibility for him own words and actions.

Most narcissists lure their victims into a trap by creating alliances. Way too soon in a relationship, the narcissist will begin talking about all the things, which the two of you have in common.

The narcissist will praise you. To the heavens and back. He will make you feel that you are seen and understood - maybe for the first time in your life. However, after a few months, things will change, and you will become the one who has to be affirmative and make him feel special.

As soon as you know this, you don't have to be on guard toward others. Surrender yourself to love and give yourself 100 %. Just bear in mind a general rule that you have to wait for one year, before you commit yourself financially and legally. Don't have children, don't buy a house, don't lend out money, and don't let anyone pay you for larger items, until you are completely sure that this person is going to treat you with respect and love.

#EXAMPLE

Lilly starts dating Peter, who has a 13-year-old daughter. It is clear that Peter is very proud of his daughter and loves her dearly. The daughter is everything to him. Peter more than insinuates that his daughter's opinion about Lilly determines whether or not Lilly and Peter's relationship will develop.

Lilly wonders, for when the daughter is there, Peter is pretty tough on her. He ridicules her, belittles her, is preachy, and only in glimpses, he acts like a father, who loves his daughter as much as he claims behind her back. Lilly tries to point it out, and Peter becomes furious. He shouts and yells, calls her names, and he gives her the cold shoulder for three days. Lilly soon learns that she shall abstain from having any opinion about Peter's relationship with his daughter.

Lilly tries to befriend the daughter. She wants to become a substitute mother because Peter had told her that her daughter's biological mother is completely mental – so Lilly reasons that the daughter needs a nice and normal grown-up female.

It isn't easy to befriend her. She feels that Peter creates obstacles every time she tries to get close to the daughter. She invites the daughter on a family trip with her own daughter, but even though everything is settled, something more important to Peter occurs on the settled date. Actually, that happens every time Lilly tries to arrange something with Peter's daughter.

However, they start talking. That's nice. One day, Lilly and the daughter sit in the living room. They are having tea, talking and laughing. Then Peter comes home and hears them laugh, talk and have fun. The next day he breaks up with Lilly. He claims that the reason is that Lilly is a bad influence on his daughter.

GASLIGHTING
– WHEN YOU ARE TOLD THAT YOU ARE IMAGINING THINGS

It is classic behavior for narcissists to use gaslighting in order to take away your confidence and your own judgment. The technique is used to undermine and distort your sense of reality.

To the narcissist, it is important that you distrust yourself because if you did trust yourself, you would never accept the narcissist's behavior – and you would never accept the narcissist's arguments in order to belittle you, take away your self-worth and confidence, and to isolate you from the friends and family members, who might have been able to support you in getting away.

The narcissist stirs things up, and then he questions your perception, when you point out all his damage – as if it doesn't exist. So, firstly the narcissist provokes your reaction, and then he denies reality and calls you crazy, hysteric, mad, squeamish and oversensitive.

The narcissist is unable to manipulate sound, sensible people, and therefore he must create a chaotic scheme of things, which will suspend normal common sense.

Why does the narcissist want to destroy you like that? Because the narcissist, when he realizes that he is not at all as wonderful, will fall down into a pain so overwhelming, that he can't stand feeling it.

Every human being with a pain too overwhelming to bear will use something inside or outside themselves in order to "carry the pain" and "feel the guilt" – and we only take another person's pain upon us, if we are brainwashed into doing so.

It is not healthy being someone who takes on guilt and pain for another person. The sound thing to do is hold the person's hand, so he can feel that he is not alone with his pain, but a narcissist will never give you that opportunity because he refuses to acknowledge the existence of the pain. He will maintain that YOU are the pain. YOU are the one hurting him; you make him react, make him violent, ridiculing, and demeaning in words and actions.

When you have been close to a narcissist, you are often skilled at recognizing when others lack empathy, are inconsiderate or don't show compassion – but you might not be good showing empathy, consideration, and compassion, either, toward yourself. When it comes to you, you are probably quite harsh: You must pull yourself together, do it better than others. You must put up with more, understand others more, and show more consideration. That is a very bad thing because you neglect to take care of yourself, like others do!

EXERCISE: QUESTIONS FOR YOURSELF

Ask yourself: "Would I treat my best friend the same way as I treat myself?" If the answer is no, you are probably too hard on yourself. It may be difficult to feel empathy toward yourself, and that's why you have to practice.

You can ask this question: "If I was the world's most loving mother/father, how would I support myself right now?"

Among other things, it is interesting that most people do know what the most loving thing to do is, but they are afraid of behaving selfishly – or rather – of being considered selfish by others. It is only healthy if your starting point first and foremost is love for yourself – and then to others This exercise helps you ask the questions which you naturally would ask a close friend, but which you might be too scared to ask yourself.

EGGSHELLS
– WHEN YOU TAKE RESPONSIBILITY FOR THE FEELINGS

Predictability. Or rather – a total lack of unpredictability. When we know what we can expect from others, we become safe and calm, and we feel free to unfold, to be creative, fun, and alive.

Do you know the expression "walking on eggshells"? If not, you will soon learn it with a narcissist. This means treading carefully without putting a foot wrong. Believe me, the narcissist will teach you soon enough! The difficulty for you lies in stopping that behavior after being free again.

The narcissist throws tantrums – and they will appear, when you least expect it, and on the basis of things which only make sense in upside-down- no-sense-at-all-universes. The narcissist can get furious, totally out of pedagogic (or any other) reach, over mealy apples, wrongly placed items in the kitchen, something on the television, or other road users. Their rage is completely out of proportion and fairness, and it hits the nearest people, if they fail to get out of the way.

This means that as a relative, you can't count on predictable stability from your narcissist, and since you can't predict the illogical and over dimensional fury, you automatically start walking on eggshells – you are careful of what you say and do because you NEVER know what triggers a fit of rage.

You begin to see yourself as someone who tries to make the narcissist's life easier, while the narcissist becomes someone, who makes your life more difficult. With a narcissist, there are always two versions of reality: The truth – and the narcissist's version of it.

Loving a person who doesn't love you is one thing. It is something else, loving a person, who seems to love you, and then realize that the person doesn't and never has. It is heartbreaking, and it shatters your concept of the world and makes you doubt everything which you thought you knew.

You can't understand what it feels like, unless you have tried it, but if you have, you know how destructive this is to your belief in everything good in this world – and to you.

It is completely wrong to claim that a narcissist can't control his fury. He is completely able to control it – when there are outsiders, who haven't been brainwashed by him, present. So, when he says: "I can't help it, when I get that furious. I can't control it," then it is a blatant lie.

#EXAMPLE

Marianne comes home with groceries from the supermarket. Poul sits on the sofa and watches a movie. He has asked her to buy apples, and she bought beautiful, red apples wrapped in a plastic bag. Poul doesn't like fruit from boxes because others might have touched it.

He gets up from the sofa; not to help Marianne unpack, but to rip the bag apart, take an apple, and look at it as if it was the prize for a marathon. He rubs the apple against his pants, so it shines, and then he takes a large bite. But instead of getting happy and content, he spits out the bite and hurls the apple straight toward Marianne, and it hits her hard on the shoulder.

Poul shouts: "For fucks sake, Marianne, you are totally incapable of doing anything right. These apples are mealy! You should have checked them out! You are doing this on purpose. You try to annoy me. I don't get it. I simply don't understand what is happening inside your little pea-brain."

Marianne is shocked, holds her breath, and pulls her shoulders up to her ears. She knows that the best strategy is standing completely still, until he calms down; then it will be over sooner than if she says something, cries, starts a discussion, or tries to walk away. Her entire body crumbles, and even though Poul's fit of rage is over ten minutes later, the shock is still in her body and makes her vulnerable for the rest of the day. She will do anything to keep him happy. That isn't easy.

The narcissist sometimes promises that "this will never happen again" – and that goes for violence, infidelity, lies, broken promises, or other forms of letdowns and abuse, but you can remain 100 % certain that it will happen.

When you try to remind the narcissist that he promised that it wouldn't, he will push the responsibility aside and blame something or someone else but himself – for his letdowns, his lies, his broken promises, his lousy treatment of you – and most of the time you will be the reason for his behavior – he will say that you just could have abstained from… [here, you can insert something innocent or fair yourself].

TAKING PITY ON THE NARCISSIST
– WHEN THEY PLAY THE VICTIM

The narcissist will use any and all methods to get you to stay and not leave them. One of the very common strategies is to make you feel sorry for them, to pity them. Whether your narcissist is a martyr narcissist, a depression narcissist, a introvert narcissist or a classic narcissist, they will from the moment you start dating, let you know that they are really victims of other people's wrongdoings. They will build an image in you that will make you try to defend them against a cruel world and support them because you feel no one else has. It makes it harder to set boundaries and exceptionally hard to leave them.

They will use their misfortune as a shield against taking responsibility, explain how nothing is their fault, they have fallen prey to abusers and frauds - and of course you owe it to them, to be there for them. They might not even say it, but just imply it. "No one cares for me. I am all alone in this world!" will make you want to comfort them and validate them and tell them that YOU are there for them.

The narcissist will tell you that you have to treat them differently and be more patient with them because:

- he had a rough childhood
- his family hates him - or at least they don't understand him
- no one understands what it's like to be him
- his boss does not see his talent
- everyone is jealous of him and his skills, looks and ideas
- his ex was a psycho
- his sister is a psycho
- his neighbour is out to get him

What you need to do is ask yourself: As an adult, should we be able to deal with stuff like that? Should he, as a grown man, be able to build a life for himself? And especially - if he is as amazing as he claims to be - how come he can't do this?

#EXAMPLE

I had a client once, who was 47 years old, a trained psychiatrist and said she needed help to raise his self confidence. He told me that all of his employers had misunderstood him and underestimated him. He had been in 24 jobs and was fired from each and everyone of them – and it was never his fault. I asked him what grounds he was fired on and it was the same in every job: he was arrogant, uncooperative and felt he knew better than everybody else.

When I asked him if there was maybe something to it – just a little bit of truth, he became very upset and spent 10 minutes defending himself, trying to make me understand that he was one of his country's most gifted psychiatrists.

#EXAMPLE

Camille felt sorry for her husband. He had put her through hell and still she couldn't leave him.

His mother and sister had mental issues, but of course he claimed to have none, he was the only sane person in the family. But the fact that his mother and sister had issues meant that he was judged from that by everyone. He couldn't have a job, because some issues with his mother or sister would always come up that he had to take care of and it was more important than any job.

Confronted with the fact that his mother and sister were grown ups and not his responsibility, he became angry, shouted and yelled at Camille for several minutes calling her cold and unempathetic. Normally he would then go to bed and stay there for a day or two, claiming he was so hurt, he could get depressed and become anorexic and it was all her fault!

She was at her wits end and had no clue how to move on and get out. Every time she would mention leaving him, he threatened to kill himself.

I asked Camille: "How does he help himself?" - because the pattern she saw him having with his mother and sister, was the same pattern she had with him. And of course another logical question for Camille was: "How do you help yourself?"

Her first step would be to reach out to me as a therapist and work from there.

FURY AND COLDNESS
– WHEN YOU BECOME POWERLESS

The narcissistic fury is a classic symptom of the disorder, but it is also a foolproof sign that the narcissist is emotionally immature. Think of a child in a supermarket. The child wants candy, and its mother or father says no. The child gets down on the floor, it screams and pounds arms and legs toward the floor, and no matter what its parents say, the fury continues. It is impossible to get through with common sense or anything else.

When the narcissist becomes furious, it happens – just like with small children – within a split second, and it is caused by something, which isn't fair or doesn't make sense for a grown-up to react furiously upon. You can't get through to a narcissist, no matter what you say or do. The difference between the child, who gets furious, and the adult narcissist, is that the adult narcissist harbors so much subconscious fear – of being revealed, of being abandoned, of failing, of not getting what is necessary in order to survive – that his reptilian brain is strongly activated, when he becomes furious.

The reptilian brain only has three ways of reaction: Flee, fight, or play dead. When the narcissist is in the middle of his rage, there is no contact with the frontal lobes, which normally would connect common sense to the thing, which annoys. The fear is simply too strong. The narcissist acts like a warrior going berserk, and there is a big risk that the narcissist will hurt you or his surroundings physically.

You might be aware that when children become furious in a way, where they are out of reach, it might be a good idea just to sit nearby without saying anything, and just be there, until it has passed. The child is able to get through its rage on its own, and find back to its parent, or take a time-out in its room. It is the same with the narcissist, BUT if you in any way feel endangered, you must remove yourself from the narcissist without taking time to explain or defend your action. Just get away.

It is unsound to be close to this fury too often. Since it appears out of the blue, doesn't make sense, and is unstoppable with common sense, YOUR reptilian brain gets activated, and you will find yourself in the same bad situation: Flee, fight, or play dead. Playing dead is when your body becomes numb and rigid from fear, and you are unable to act; or your body falls apart like a wet cloth, and you lose control over your feet, so you can't get away.

The reptilian brain is designed to save your life when facing a life-threatening situation, but when the fury comes out of the blue, it is often too late to flee, and therefore you might "freeze".

When threatened by a predator, it might be a clever move to lie down and play dead, but when facing the narcissistic fury, your body gets tense, and in the future, you will be on guard, maybe without realizing it, and that means that your body produces cortisol – the stress hormone – and your body is in an everlasting state of stress. Nobody can stand up to that pressure in the end, and at some point, the long-term symptoms of stress affect your health.

Some narcissists display the narcissistic fury as ice-cold, closed rejection, where the narcissist freezes you out, both verbally and with their body language. You will clearly know that you are the one being frozen out.

Our body contains something called mirror neurons. They react to other peoples' body language, while our brain at the same time reads thousands of messages from our surroundings. Therefore, you will never doubt that you are the one in the wrong – according to the narcissist.

When someone is cocksure and opinionated, we tend to become insecure, and that is what happens here. You will doubt whether you are the one being in the wrong in this conflict. You may feel powerless and unable to react – and act. You might feel like a victim or a hostage.

Children are rarely capable of acting toward a narcissistic parent, who is infuriated or acting cold as ice. However, you are an adult, and you can do something. You can remove yourself from the other person straight away. You can choose to understand that narcissism is a disease, and that this is not to be taken personally; while remembering that the narcissist is desperate and feels powerless.

The intent of the fury and the coldness is – unconsciously – to transfer those feelings to YOU instead of the narcissist.

What you may forget is asking yourself: "Is this proper behavior? Is it OK to be that furious or freeze somebody out? Would I accept that kind of behavior from my best friend?" If the answer is no, you have to focus on that instead of the content of the behavior or the cause of it. Stick to the point: This is not okay.

You can't change the narcissist's behavior. He will probably think that this is your own fault – that your actions cause him to behave like that. So, you might try asking yourself: "If I am the one to take care of me, how can I do it the best possible way, when something like this happens?"

#EXAMPLE

When Charlotte met her boyfriend, she thought that she was suffering from lactose intolerance. Since her early teens, she had often suffered from an aching and bloated stomach. Her doctor was unable to find out what caused it. Her mother, Inge, had a self- diagnosed lactose intolerance herself, and this meant a great deal for her mother, since it was something that mother and daughter had in common.

Charlotte's boyfriend was a medical student, and he soon realized that Charlotte didn't suffer from lactose intolerance, but often reacted to instability; especially when she and her mother had a clash.

Charlotte felt happy and relieved because it meant that she again was able to eat cheese, chocolate, and ice cream, and as soon as Charlotte realized what the symptoms were about, they disappeared. At that time, Charlotte and her parents were on relatively good terms, and Charlotte made a happy phone- call home, but she was very careful not to mention the parents as the cause of her stomach aches. She just referred to general uneasiness and instability.

Her mother got all quiet on the phone, but she didn't say anything. A few days later, all hell broke loose.

During a drive with her father, he ordered her to break up with her boyfriend because "he claims that you are mentally ill."

When Charlotte replied that he never had said anything like it, her father continued: "Yes, he does because your mother has told me about the lactose intolerance. Your boyfriend point-blank says that you have a psychic reaction, and then you ARE mentally ill. You just have to get away from him because when the two of you get married and have children, and you then are going to get a divorce, he can claim custody over the children by stating that you are mentally ill."

Charlotte was shocked that her parents had managed to come up with that story together: That a man, whom Charlotte had only dated for a few months, suddenly wanted to marry her and have children, just in order to claim sole custody at the apparently inevitable divorce. It seemed completely insane.

Charlotte continued: "Can't you even hear how ridiculous this sounds?" she asked. "We don't even live together, we have just met, and now the two of you are talking about children and divorce?"

Her parents' statement became even more grotesque seen in the light of a situation one month earlier, when Charlotte's mother had scolded her for using birth control pills because she meant that Charlotte would get cancer and will be unable to bear children.

The demonization of Charlotte's boyfriend began early. Normally, Charlotte's mother would cast the bullets, and when she was prevented from it herself, Charlotte's father would fire them for her. After that episode, her parents again acted with total silence, until her mother one day called and once again acted like nothing had happened. Charlotte ended up cutting off the contact with her parents.

#EXAMPLE

Michael and Brigitte have a conflict. Michael becomes furious and throws dinner plates at Brigitte while yelling at her and she ducks and tries to calm him down, which just makes him even more furious. One time a dinner plate hits her in the forehead and she has to get stitches. After she comes home, she tries to talk to him about it, but he deflects - he doesn't want to talk about it. When she insists, he says it was her own fault; he is allowed to be angry and she could just have ducked or gotten out of the way. Michael gets really angry at being blamed and confronted and threatens to leave her if she won't apologize and he doesn't talk to her for three days, no matter what she says. In the end, she apologizes out of fear of being alone.

GUILT AND SHAME
– WHEN YOU ARE CAUSING THE BAD BEHAVIOR

If there was an annual, international award for making other people feel guilty and shameful, the narcissists would win – every year. The narcissists are able to make you feel shameful about the most ridiculous things – even just being you. They can make you feel that YOU owe them something, even when they treat you badly.

The narcissist makes you feel that you are a bad person, if you are unable to look above your own needs – and the needs you have to fulfill belong to the narcissist. As the narcissist says: "You know, you have to do something for others and not just think about yourself." The narcissist will never understand that he is doing exactly what he accuses you of doing – i.e. projection. This means letting others take the blame or being the cause of something we have done (or haven't done).

#EXAMPLE

Jonn's parents had to marry earlier than planned because Jonn's mother was pregnant with Jonn. Every time Jonn's parents have a fight, and they often do, his father tells him that if Jonn hadn't been born, his father wouldn't have had to marry, and he wouldn't have to live in such a hell.

Jonn feels that he is to blame for his parent's arguments and bad marriage, and he takes great care to not cause further reasons for them to be angry with him – he thinks that he has caused enough misery. Evidently, it is an excuse for two people to blame a third person – and even their own child – for their own miserable life. It is caused by their choices and their lacking ability to take responsibility, not by the presence of a child – but this is precisely how the narcissistic way of thinking works.

From very early on in the relations, the narcissist's relatives are made emotionally and existentially responsible for the narcissist's well-being. When it comes to romantic relationships, it begins in a positive way: "I become a better person with you in my life." "I am always happy, when I am with you." Or: "I don't need anybody else in my life but you." We like to feel important – it is a basic human condition – and then it is easy to overlook how we are made responsible for the other person's well-being. It follows that we are also responsible, if the other person is cross, annoyed, dissatisfied, and in a bad mood. We feel guilty without being able to understand why.

THE NARCISSIST BLAMES YOU FOR BEING LAZY, SELFISH, LYING, IRRESPONSIBLE, AND FAKE, BUT IT IS EVIDENT THAT IT IS IN FACT HIM WHO IS ALL OF THOSE THINGS. IT IS CALLED "PROJECTION". LIKE A PROJECTOR THROWS AN IMAGE ON A WALL, THE NARCISSIST PROJECTS HIS OWN WORST CHARACTERISTICS ONTO YOU. HE IS DOING

THIS SO HE DOESN'T HAVE TO CONTAIN THEM AND TAKE
RESPONSIBILITY FOR THEM HIMSELF. HE FEELS BETTER,
IF YOU DO IT.
IT SEEMS TOTALLY SURREAL!

#EXAMPLE

Often, the narcissist is very cunning. Larna and Loui entered therapy after Loui had called me and persistently claimed that he was to blame for Larna's depression and anxiety. When I asked him exactly how he could cause this, he couldn't tell me, but said that Larna had told him so many times.

When he asked her why she was sad, she said that it was because of him. It sounded suspiciously familiar.

Obviously, an alarm bell should sound, so you remember that it takes two to tango. Or, think that Larna was a narcissist, who projected the guilt toward Loui.

However, something in Loui's explanations and allegations set my alarm bells ringing. I asked him: "If you don't know what you are doing to make Larna feel so unhappy, how can you accept the premise that you are the guilty one?"

He couldn't answer that, but when I asked him to ask her directly, she had replied that he overstepped her boundaries, and that he kept lying to her.

I asked them to join me for a session of marriage counseling, and there Larna provided numerous examples of how Loui manipulated, threatened her, was violent, lied, and overstepped her boundaries. Larna felt guilty because she had said "I do – 'till death do us part", and because she felt that she ought to love him, when he clearly loved her and really wanted them to stay together.

He, on the other hand, thought that she should pull herself together, love him, and stay happy. He was low on empathy, even when he was confronted with situations, like when he had pulled Larna through the house by her hair – with the children witnessing it, and he said: "But I DID apologize – can't we just move on?!"

The formal definition of shame is a sense of pain deriving from the experience of having lost others' respect due to unsuitable behavior; to actions incompatible with the values of a certain culture, or the feeling of being marked as useless and unlovable. Shame is the feeling of disgrace originating from something regrettable, unfortunate, or disgraceful.

Adults don't need guilt and shame, at all. Really. We know the difference between right and wrong – and if we don't, we are probably not ashamed of it.

If we are mentally sane, we are able to recognize, when another person feels trampled on, without turning shameful and guilty ourselves – and we can see, when it really IS our responsibility.

Therefore, guilt and shame are something, which we should happily let go, and that is extremely difficult for relatives of narcissists.

Guilt and shame provoke different reactions within us. Shame gives us an oppressive feeling inside our body, and it can stir up feelings of deep mourning or low self-worth. Guilt can also cause anger because we feel exposed, or as victims of our own weakness.

Both reactions can make us feel worthless, hopeless, or helpless. These feelings can again lead to depression, anxiety, and many other damaging feelings and physical illnesses – for instance stress reactions caused by the feeling of being wrong and out-of-place.

Guilt and shame can cause an endless number of negative thoughts and excessive thoughts, which steal your peace of mind.

As long as you stick to the feelings of guilt and shame you will never acquire emotional freedom, strength, or health – neither mentally, nor physically.

Guilt, shame, and bad conscience are mechanisms used in order to raise a child to fit into a certain culture.

The sounder that culture is, the less it is necessary to use guilt, shame, and bad conscience (which essentially is the same as guilt, we are just more familiar with the term "guilty conscience", and from now on I will refer to it as guilt and shame; just so you know what I mean by it).

Guilt and shame become basic feelings, which prevent you from moving on because you feel that this would be a selfish act.

DID YOU KNOW THIS?
DID YOU KNOW THAT THE GUILT AND SHAME, WHICH YOU CARRY AROUND, ARE UNNECESSARY, AND THEY NEITHER TEACH YOU ANYTHING, NOR KEEP YOU ON THE NARROW PATH OF VIRTUE, NOR MAKE YOU HAPPIER OR CALMER? TRY REFLECTING ON THIS:
"WHAT WOULD I DO TODAY/THIS YEAR/IN THIS LIFE GENERALLY, IF I DIDN'T FEEL GUILTY OR ASHAMED?"

THE SPIDER
– WHEN THE NARCISSIST CONTROLS THE SURROUNDINGS

The narcissist compares to the vampire, but also the spider, which weaves its beautiful, tangled web, and then sits in a corner waiting for prey. When the dew falls upon the threads, they glisten in the sun and attract other animals getting caught in the web. The spider hurls forward and poisons the victim, so it dissolves from within, and then the spider weaves a cocoon around the victim and waits for the poison to work, until the spider can devour its victim as a good, hot porridge on a cold day.

We, too, are poisoned by the narcissist. When we have fallen for the "dew" – the tender words and the attention, we become gaslighted and start doubting our own perception of the reality. We doubt whether we have any right to be a part of this world, at all. We become invisible, and we dissolve.

A spider's web is just like a wheel with spokes radiating from the hub. In the narcissist's family, the narcissist has taken the place of the hub, and the spokes separate the family members from one another.

No one must get too close to each other; and definitely not closer to anyone but the narcissist, who likes to keep his victims close; even though they never really get access to his deepest and most inner secrets – primarily because the narcissist doesn't have access to that area, either.

THE COSTS OF LOVING A NARCISSIST:
MENTALLY, YOU LOSE YOUR COMMON SENSE, YOUR SELF-WORTH, AND YOUR CONFIDENCE.
PHYSICALLY, IT COSTS YOUR ENERGY AND YOUR GOOD HEALTH.
EMOTIONALLY, YOU PAY WITH FEAR, DEPRESSION, AND ANXIETY.
SOUL-WISE, YOU SACRIFICE YOURSELF AND YOUR SOUL.
SOCIALLY, YOU RISK YOUR JOB, YOUR NETWORK, AND THE SUPPORT FROM YOUR FRIENDS.
SEXUALLY, THE PRICE IS YOUR JOY, LOVE, AND CONFIDENCE IN OTHERS AND YOURSELF.

#EXAMPLE

Matthew is a middle manager in a large company. His equals have split opinions about him, but he is highly favored among the superiors. The subordinates seem to agree that you never really know about Matthew, but that he must be good at his work, since he holds that position in the company.

When Matthew is going to solve a task, there is no limit to his visions and ideas, and he is very good at getting the right persons attached to the project.

Matthew is very charming, and he is always optimistic. He tells the individual co-worker that his or her particular effort is invaluable to the project, but from other colleagues the co-workers hear that Matthew has talked behind their backs and said that they delay the project.

Somehow, Matthew's projects almost always succeed. He rarely contributes himself, but he manipulates the co-workers to do almost all the work. Naturally, Matthew takes the entire credit. When a project fails, he knows precisely who to blame, so he stays out of trouble with the superiors. He controls his projects and the involved co-workers with a mixture of fear and charm.

SPLITTING, THE GOLDEN CHILD AND THE BLACK SHEEP
- WHEN YOU HAVE BEEN CHOSEN OR OSTRACIZED

Splitting is when the narcissist poisons all members of the family, a group of workers, or a group of friends, so they don't trust each other. When trust is absent, they can't form a connection and rebel against the narcissist.

Even though the narcissists often are unaware that they are doing this, it is a very effective power tool. The narcissist will lie about the individual members of the family or group, thus ensuring that no one trusts the others. As such, that is a crazy approach, since confidence in family members, colleagues, and friends is immensely important to all of us, if we are going to perform optimally, grow as human beings, or give our love to others.

A part of the splitting is when the narcissist provides the others with incorrect and false roles – but for instance, children will believe in them because children always cooperate with their parents. Tell the children that they are stupid, and they will become stupid. Tell them that they are something special and above others, and they will act that way – not because they are stupid or bad, but because children do what is necessary in order to survive and get even a tiny piece of recognition when they live up to their parents' expectations. The most well-known roles are "The Golden Child" and "The Black Sheep/Scapegoat".

#EXAMPLE

Ellen has two sons, Poul and Jørgen. Throughout their upbringing, she repeatedly drags them aside and tells them, individually, that: "You can't trust your brother, he doesn't want what is best for you. You can't confide in him; he will stab you in the back!"

Ellen works with splitting, and the two boys never become friends. Whenever they meet, they argue and yell at each other, and they accuse each other for being disloyal and unkind. At the same time, Ellen points out one on behalf of the other. For instance, when Poul has had a bath, she pulls Jørgen out into the bathroom and says: "Look, Jørgen. When Poul has bathed, it is almost impossible to see traces of it afterwards. You might take a leaf out of your brother's book!"

Jørgen feels that he is unable to live up to her expectations without being a copy of his brother, and that causes huge problems, since the brothers have very different personalities. Jørgen spends most of his life trying to be good enough, and he fights a massive drinking problem.

Poul – the golden child – carries sky-high expectations – and at the same time he feels that his mother isn't proud of him or loves him, but that she just sees him as a sort of performance. And, he has to live up to that in order not to be frozen out by her ice-cold attitude, when she is dissatisfied with him. His entire life he struggles to perform more than others, and he develops into a narcissistic adult, who never grows content with himself or others.

It is no blessing being the golden child. Many people think that being the favorite is a good thing, but it is neither easy nor comfortable. It feels like being a donkey, who is harnessed to a stick with a carrot – and the carrot moves seventy miles per hour.

These mechanisms occur among both friends, lovers and colleagues. In the workplace, you will experience that the narcissist points out someone on your behalf, thus making you feel that you are not good enough. You are unable to protest; if you did, you would be accused of being jealous.

Even if you say in a straightforward manner: "I sense that you are calling attention to the other person to make me perform better, or to make me feel that I am not doing it good enough," you will just be accused of being paranoid.

Or, the narcissist will try to form alliances by contacting you behind your colleagues' backs in order to ensure that you support him.

#EXAMPLE

Eric is the president of an association. Before every meeting, he calls the other board members, one by one, to make sure that they have been fed with his arguments for or against the various topics, and that they agree with him. Besides getting his own way, she appears to be someone who unites the board, and who hinders endless discussions at the meetings – well, he has already done the work – so they are able to carry through more important issues under his presidency. He appears to be a very competent and efficient leader.

However, he also tells every board member that exactly THAT person is someone special, and that he feels particularly connected with and understood by that person. Gradually, he makes them yield because they feel special and important. He also tells them that the others are not nearly as skillful and intelligent as the person he is speaking with.

If he discovers that the others have been talking to each other about something behind HIS back, he uses guilt as a weapon: "Why did you talk to Karen about it? I thought that we had a deal! I don't find this move particularly clever. We are wasting time, whenever you do something like this."

NARCISSISTS PROVIDE YOU WITH GUILT AND SHAME
THROUGH EMOTIONAL BLACKMAIL AND MANIPULATION:
- THEY GIVE YOU ULTIMATUMS.
- THEY USE TEARS AGAINST YOU.
- THEY GIVE YOU THE COLD SHOULDER.
- THEY PLAY VICTIMS.
- THEY MAKE YOU SEE THEM AS VULNERABLE PEOPLE
NEEDING SPECIAL CONSIDERATION.
- THEY MAKE YOU FEEL GUILTY.
- THEY MAKE YOU FEEL ASHAMED.

The narcissistic parent **will** force his children to choose sides and involve them in the family dramas. The narcissist will do "splitting". He will cause bad blood between the family members, and they are never going to truly trust one another. It is a part of the tactic – subconsciously, of course – to ensure that those close to the narcissist will never form alliances AGAINST the narcissist.

It is typical for a narcissistic family and for a workplace with a narcissistic superior to contain a huge amount of mistrust, unspoken words, and unfinished conflicts because no one trusts anyone. In workplaces, it often shows when the manager sets the employees against each other.

#EXAMPLE

Ellen (from the previous example) bore two boys five years apart. She tells both of them, when the other is out of reach: "You can't trust your brother. He is kind enough, he just doesn't act for your good," and she continuously praises one of the brothers and not the other – as if the youngest son should be able to do the same as his five-year older brother.

The youngest feels inferior and has many complexes, and he starts hating his older brother – and that goes on throughout both their lives, since they can't talk to each other about it because their mother has impressed them with mutual distrust!

Whenever they are together, they argue, get into physical fights, yell at and threaten each other. Their mother has efficiently taught them to hate each other without ever telling them to do so. In that way, the sons are unable to put on a united front against her, and that is a classic trait for both narcissists and psychopaths. They divide other people, so they don't risk being met with a united family or group.

THE OMNISCIENT NARCISSIST
– WHEN YOU ARE BEING PUT DOWN

Narcissists are above general law and other rules. They resent when others break them, but narcissists feel above others, and they are convinced that it is of no consequence, when THEY don't follow them. After all, laws and rules are made for ORDINARY people to follow. That is necessary, of course. But narcissists feel special. They are more in the right than others, and they have the right to do whatever they want.

If you wish to provoke a reaction from a narcissist, you only have to make it clear that he is just as ordinary as other completely ordinary people.

Nothing special. Or point out that he doesn't have special rights compared to others. Then you just have to wait for a great display of fireworks filled with objections, evasions, bad excuses, and, sometimes, fury.

NARCISSISTS HAVE TWO SET OF RULES:

1. **RULES FOR YOU:**
   YOU MUST TAKE RESPONSIBILITY FOR MISTAKES.
   YOU MUST APOLOGIZE. YOU MUST NOT CRITICIZE. YOU
   MUST RESPECT THEM.
   YOU MUST DO WHAT THEY LIKE.
   YOU MUST THINK WHAT THEY THINK.
   YOUR FEELINGS ARE UNIMPORTANT AND INVALID.

2. **RULES FOR NARCISSISTS: NO RULES APPLY TO NARCISSISTS.**

#EXAMPLE
Kim is a highly educated specialist, but his résumé contains 22 different jobs in only 14 years.

Kim states the reason is that he is too skilled. His colleagues or his bosses are always jealous of his abilities, and they want to get rid of him. They are too stupid. They don't understand his talent. They fail to appreciate his exceptional competence. They are afraid of his capability.

A man of his caliber needs challenges. The superiors are narrow minded
Kim enters therapy, but she is unable to accept that the many job changes
have anything to do with him. Kim is a narcissist.

GHOSTING
– WHEN YOU ARE GIVEN THE COLD SHOULDER

Ghosting is when someone stops answering your letters, your phone calls, or your social media messages. Without a cause. It is as if the person disappears, and no matter WHAT you write, there is no reaction. And then, suddenly, he is back.

When you want to confront him with the lacking communication, he will act surprised and appalled, and say things like: "Ah, really! Had I known that you were that vulnerable/needy/intense, then I … [insert any lame answer here]" or "Yes, but work, you know. That's important. You don't want me to ignore my job, do you?" – like in: "Do you really think that you are just as important as anything else in my life?! No!"

Even though you clearly state that regular communication and just a tiny reply on your messages are important to you, this pattern is going to repeat itself, for he has done it once and seen that it works. So, now this method has been added to his list of useful weapons – and he is going to use it, when you least expect it!

Unfortunately, ghosting has become common usage for a large part of the population, whenever the interest for another person fades away. That is not a sound behavior.

If you have dated someone for a while and wish to put an end to it, you have to take responsibility and say: "I am no longer interested," so you don't leave the other person in an emotional vacuum. However, ghosting is much more than just refraining from answering.

When ghosting becomes a truly unhealthy behavior as a part of a personality disorder, it can be used to control another person.

Ghosting is NOT the same as when you go no contact with the narcissist. Ghosting happens for no reason, lasts for a period and at times where everything seems fine - just to make you insecure.

#EXAMPLE

Nina met Palle on a dating website, and they have been dating on and off for a month. They kiss, hug, and hold hands, and Nina plans on making their first real lovemaking something special. She books a romantic weekend getaway, and the two lovebirds have a wonderful weekend with hot love, many kisses, tender words, and promises.

After the weekend, Nina floats on cloud nine, and Monday morning she sends a cute little message to Palle, expecting another back, but hears nothing from him. In the evening, she writes again, but she has to go to bed without any reaction.

Her brain starts processing why he isn't replying, and she tries telling herself that he is just very busy at work, but her brain doesn't seem to accept it, and she doesn't get much sleep that night. Why doesn't he answer her? Just a little "hello and kisses"? They were doing so well together.

The next day, she writes to him again – both on SMS and Messenger – and she records a small message on his answering machine. There is still no answer.

Tuesday evening, she writes to tell him that she is a bit frustrated over the lack of even just a small message, but still no reaction.

Wednesday – after two sleepless nights – she is getting crazy. She thinks about contacting him in his workplace – maybe he lost his phone? Maybe something has happened to him?

Suddenly she gets a Facebook notification. Palle has uploaded a photo of himself sitting in a café by the water with a glass of wine. But it isn't a selfie – someone else has taken the shot, and he smiles sweetly at the camera, as if it is a special person behind it.

Nina gets very upset. She calls him and leaves a message telling him to let her know if he has regrets, or if he has met someone else – she just needs to know what is going on!

That is Palle's "clue". Now he knows that he has got her right where he wants her. Then he writes to her on Messenger: "Hi Nina, thank you for a nice weekend. You are so wonderful. See you later."

He gives her a chunk of meat, but not enough for her to be satisfied, since he doesn't explain his lack of messages for almost three days. Palle suggests that they meet up the following weekend, and Nina agrees to it.

When they meet, Nina tries to make Palle explain why he was unable to message her, but he seems surprised and says that he had such a wonderful weekend, so he was convinced that it was all right for him to spend some time on his work. But maybe she disagrees?

Nina has to agree with him, she has no other option. When she asks him about the photographer, he says that it was just a colleague. When Nina says that she wishes that she was the one who sat there and drank wine with him, he asks her whether she has a tendency toward jealousy!

FALSE CONFIDENTIALITY
– WHEN THE NARCISSIST ABUSES YOUR WEAKNESS

In the beginning of your relation, the narcissist will create an alliance, which makes it easy for you to confide in him – about yourself, your close ones, your innermost thoughts, dreams, and maybe even your weaknesses. That is also the case in a healthy relationship, but there, both parties confide in each other, and they are both very open as to who they really are.

Often, in a relationship with a narcissist, you will be the only one opening up, and you can be absolutely certain that anything you say will be used against you in a conflict later, or as an argument for the reason why the narcissist is innocent.

#EXAMPLE

Linda has a new boss whom she really likes. The boss includes Linda in many decisions, invites Linda and her family home for dinner, and expresses that Linda is a valuable employee within the company.

They have also talked about family matters, and the boss has asked about Linda's background. Linda told him that she was placed in a foster family as a child.

Some months later, everyone in the company is busy, and Linda feels under pressure because she senses that her boss fails to fulfill the contractor deals. When Linda carefully asks about the specific contracts, the boss gets infuriated and abuses Linda's confidentiality against her by saying that "you obviously see letdowns and mistrust everywhere because of your childhood."

COPYCATTING
– WHEN THE NARCISSIST STEALS YOUR LIFE

Narcissism is one of three personality disorders within the same category. The other two are psychopathy and sociopathy.

The psychopaths are cold as ice, and they are very well aware of what they do and say but think that they are above everyone else, so they have the right to do everything – and they stand by it; contrary to the narcissist who will always explain his bad behavior away.

In short, the sociopath is known for being a chameleon. He copies other peoples' lives, and then he pushes the victim away and takes over the victim's place.

People and diagnoses are not solid boxes which we can fit each other into and therefore we can recognize characteristics from both the psychopath and the sociopath when it comes to narcissistic behavior. It might confuse, but it still makes sense, since the three diagnoses belong to the same category.

#EXAMPLE

Ann works for Adam, who is a painter. She receives a 30% fee for planning his exhibitions and taking care of the administrative work. Their relation is purely work related; Ann is homosexual and lives with her partner of many years, and Adam has a wife.

Adam has some narcissistic characteristics. Out of the blue or caused by trifles, he can become infuriated with Ann. Even though Ann works hard for him, and he is successful and sells many paintings, he often accuses her for not doing enough for him. It is as if she always fails to do things good enough.

At other times, Adam behaves like Ann is the only one who really understands him, and he is so grateful for her work, and he tells her that she is the source of his success. When Ann says that he has created the success himself because he is a great painter, he agrees with her and laughs coyly. There is never an in-between with him. Adam is either mad about Ann and her work, or very unsatisfied and frustrated.

In the beginning, Ann was pretty frustrated about this; until she found some descriptions of narcissists, psychopaths, and sociopaths. Adam carries characteristics from each of the three personality disorders.

They are Facebook friends, and after a while Ann realizes that Adam often posts when she does. If she puts something up, so does he within one hour. It doesn't stop there. He often posts similar content to her posts. It is often a characteristic from the sociopathic personality disorder, but as mentioned, diagnoses are not solid boxes which we fit into and therefore we often recognize characteristics from various personality disorders within the same person.

When Ann writes something about her partner, Jessie, then Adam for certain will write something about his wife. When Ann writes about work, Adam writes something work-related after a short while.

Presumably, Adam doesn't see it himself, but maybe he feels compelled to compete. He sees something in Ann's life which he wants – and that is a common characteristic of all three personality disorders. They all want what others have – and they are unaware of it. Adam's reaction is sociopathic. The narcissist wishes to get closer and then tear Ann's self-worth apart – caused by a subconscious envy.

After about six months, Ann casually says that she has noticed that they often inspire each other since they often post the same content. Adam denies it, and he says that he hasn't noticed, and that their relation is not THAT close. He laughs it off and says that if he didn't know that Ann was a dyke, he would suspect that she was coming on to him.

She protests carefully against being called a dyke, and he calls her squeamish and petit bourgeois, and he asks if she has lost her sense of humor.

The following day, Adam writes an update about people without any sense of humor, and how little respect he has toward those people. He doesn't mention Ann, but she is able to read between the lines, and she also realizes that he would deny that it had anything to do with her if she confronted him.

Flying Monkeys – When Even Your Closest Relations Don't Understand

CAN'T YOU JUST TALK ABOUT IT?

"But you must be able to talk to each other?!" "Perhaps you are a bit too sensitive?!"

"He is probably just a bit stressed. I am sure that he has no bad intentions!"

"Ahh, he is definitely not out to harm you."

"I am sure that you have misunderstood something."

In the beginning, when you tell your family and friends about this amaaaaazing new partner/colleague/boss, they are happy for you – maybe they even feel a bit jealous, since your descriptions leave no doubt that this is a fairytale relationship. You are head over heels, and everything is possible. Besides, when they meet this person, they will get praise, acknowledgment and flattery. This behavior "softens" them, and subconsciously they place the narcissist on a pedestal – and when you are there, no one can reach you. Therefore, when you tell your friends that things don't look so wonderful anymore, it goes wrong.

It doesn't help you that the narcissist probably already has begun brainwashing you into believing that everything is your fault. So, when your closest allies doubt your experiences, you will wonder yourself, whether you are overreacting, imagining things, or misinterpreting it.

People, who without knowing contribute to your own distrust, are called "flying monkeys". The monkeys fly through the air, swing in the vines, grab your glasses, and disappear with them before you know it. The monkeys are not evil; this is just the way they are. They don't understand how important your glasses are, and how they help you see clearly. The expression derives from the film The Wizard of Oz, where the flying monkeys are called winged monkeys.

#EXAMPLE

After the break between Charlotte and her parents, she experienced that some of her friends and others around her didn't believe that the relationship with her parents could be that tough, since they always appeared to be a happy, organized, model family. "Yes, but all families argue, and then the family members get together again!" or "Are you sure that it is that bad?" and "Can't you just call them?" were some of the most frequent comments.

These comments show the most transgressive behavior when you are addressing a person in such a situation. If things were that easy, you would just get in touch. If this was a normal family, both sides would try

to reconcile; but in a family with a narcissistic person, things don't work that way.

Sometimes, Charlotte had the feeling of being part of a surreal, endless soap opera because everything that happened seemed so outrageous.

NARCISSISTS, ADDICTS AND ADDICTION

It may be difficult to see the difference between a narcissist and an addict because the core problems of both are denial and a lacking ability to handle their own pain. For both groups, their whole existence, everything they do, and everything they say, relate to not feeling pain and not taking responsibility. It is easier to inflict pain on others, even though it is the addict or the narcissist who inflicts that pain.

The narcissist is an addict, too. He abuses people. He is addicted – to attention. If he can't get any positive attention, he will happily take the negative.

Anyone who has been close to a narcissist must either become like him, i.e. narcissistic, or become co-dependent; i.e. addicted to and dependent on the narcissist. Even after you have left that person, you might long for what you had; just like an addict misses his drugs.

Like the addict's partner, you will start making excuses for your narcissist, and tell others that they don't know him when they tell you that they don't think that he is good for you. And, you will pull yourself away from those people, which makes it easier for the narcissist to isolate you when you tell him what your friends say. He will tell you that they don't understand how wonderful you are, and that they are jealous and don't want good things to happen to you.

In that way, the narcissist appears as a hero, and your friends and your family, who try to drag you away from that person, appear to be the enemy. You stop seeing them, and you stop telling them about the abuse, you become quiet, and you withdraw from them.

When you don't have any confidants, it is easier to abuse and violate you because there is no one there to tell you that it isn't your own fault.

Just like an addict, the narcissist expects you to stay loyal instead of honest; that you keep the secret about what is happening behind closed curtains, and that you publicly display a façade of happiness.

However, just as it doesn't help the co-dependent or the addict to hide anything, it doesn't help the narcissists and their relations, either.

THE NARCISSIST'S MASKS

The narcissist is like the classic vampire from the horror stories. The vampire transforms into a hypnotizing handsome man, who gets himself invited into your home, and then sucks your blood without you noticing it – night after night, he sinks his teeth deep into your throat and drinks your life, until you are empty and dead.

The narcissist masks as a beautiful person because he makes YOU appear as a beautiful human being, and sneakily, he "invites himself inside" – you want him in your life and in your heart. As a sneak thief, he slowly and imperceptibly breaks down your personality, and he drains you of energy and strength until you have become empty and invisible.

If you try to set boundaries for the narcissist, he is going to cross them with the argument that he has been good, kind, and considerate before – as if that is an argument for not respecting your limits. "I have been kind for such a long time, so now I can…" – as if crossing your boundaries is a reward for not directly violating you.

"What if I WAS the one being wrong? If it WAS me, who didn't love him enough? Gave enough? Was I kind enough? What if it IS me, who is crazy and mental?"

That's the way many relatives of narcissists think. They do so as a result of manipulation, verbal abuse, brainwashing, and emotional rape.

The rape victim should never take the blame for being raped. Never. When you have been exploited by a narcissist, you are not to blame for him picking you or mistreating you, either. Never.

The narcissist is unable to improve himself. He can't be cured. He can't understand what you are trying to explain. Only he, who himself recognizes that something in his behavior and communication needs changing, is susceptible to help. The narcissist will never recognize that he is in the wrong and needs to change. There is nothing the matter with him. Only with the others, and they need therapy, not him.

One of the challenges when leaving a narcissistic partner is that YOU also have become an addict. You have become addicted to the drama, the tender words, the dopamine and the adrenaline, which your body releases when you are together with the narcissist. Therefore, the ex-partners sometimes feel totally insane because they KNOW that the relationship is bad for them – and at the same time, they miss it and long for it. Well, it IS like narcotics.

Anyone who has been together with a narcissist knows that the good and beautiful moments only happen in the beginning – and later on only in glimpses in order to keep you. The narcissist only provides enough for you to stay.

I recommend that you write down concrete examples of bad experiences. Make a list; put it on your fridge, and when you feel the urge to return to your "dud" – then go and read your fridge list.

**NO, YOU DON'T MISS THE NARCISSIST.
YOU MISS THE PICTURE POSTCARD,
WHICH THE NARCISSIST PAINTED FOR YOU.**

#EXAMPLE

Shery has left Jasper. He hit her, and accused her of being the reason why he didn't succeed as an actor – and many other violations which the relatives must endure.

Shery enters therapy. She feels that she is becoming mad, she says. Even though the last months of the relationship with Jasper didn't bring anything nice or good, she constantly speculates ways to resume the relationship. She doesn't sleep at night, and she considers calling him and simply just to take full responsibility for the dysfunctional relationship.

Maybe THAT will make Jasper realize that she really means it, and he will give her the same love as he did during the first months of their romance.

She wishes that Jasper would call her and tell her that he finally realized that he treated her badly, and that they can start over and be happy together.

That is never going to happen, and it can be difficult to understand. Shery's brain is triggered with dependency to Jasper, and she is not thinking straight.

She needs to use breathing exercises, mindfulness and fridge lists to help herself stay away from Jasper.

AM I GOING MAD?

Do you know the feeling that your perception of the reality is distorted? That you can't figure out whether things happened as you thought they did – or if they really were as dramatic at the time?

When you tell others the stories, do they suddenly seem unlikely or trivial? How could such a small event explode into that drama? You sense that you are too sensitive without knowing why you feel that way.

When you ask the narcissist about the episode, the person either can't recall it or makes light of it, or maybe even accuses you of lying. On the other hand, small episodes which you didn't see as a problem, can be blown completely out of proportion even long after they took place. Maybe you made a joke, which offended the narcissist. You can be certain that he remembers it.

The narcissist memorizes every little episode he can use against you, but he "forgets" all the times he did something. A narcissist has no "right" or "wrong" as other people know it, and therefore you will feel that you play an unwilling part in an absurd theater, where the rules keep changing.

#EXAMPLE

Mariah, aged 34, decides to confront her father with all those let-downs and violations. Mariah sits down and tells him that she wishes to complete her message, before her father answers – and even though her father's facial expression turns impatient and restless, he accepts.

Mariah tells him how SHE experienced the episodes. She takes great care not "to call her father anything" or say anything which involves words that might provoke her father. Just like a lawyer, she presents her case in a sober and matter of fact-like way.

She spends about seven minutes, since she knows that this time is the range for her father's patience.

Conclusively, she says: "I have experienced those violations and let-downs, and I wish that you understand and recognize what it was like being me."

Her father is quiet while he observes Mariah, who on her part tries to guess what is going on behind her father's smooth façade, but without any luck. Finally, her father says: "What about parental let-downs? No one ever talks about that! It is extremely hard being a parent – especially when your child is as impossible as you were. Who is going to recognize MY experience?!" Her father waits for a short while as he looks reproachfully at Mariah. Then he stands up and says that he is hungry, and that they have to talk another day.

Consequences Of Long Term Relationships With A Narcissist

THE TENSIONS STICK

When we grow up in a childhood filled with insecurity, violations and traumas - or we have a long abusive relationship, we either go into "high alert" or "low alert". Either we are constantly on guard, ready for a fight, and everything happens at a high pace, i.e. high alert; or we do the opposite and get low alert by becoming evasive and slacking, and everything we do is in the last minute, too late, or not at all, i.e. low alert.

Even though it doesn't look that way, both reactions are a way of controlling the world. It is an attempt to set the agenda in a world which we really don't understand.

Traumas ALWAYS get stuck inside your body. It becomes a little bit tense and stressed; or it gets slack and energy lacking.

We are tense and on guard, and in reality, we constantly carry around stress.

When this happens, our muscles are tense. They are ready for fight or flight. Even when we are intimate with others. Even when we are having sex, which is supposed to be that activity where we should be most devoted and vulnerable and open.

When you are tense that way, there isn't much room for pleasure and devotion. Your entire system is occupied with something else – that the world is a dangerous place, and your body shuts down for anything which doesn't concern that fight, and then you become unable to feel anything else.

Since we are programmed for survival, we become someone who walks around tense instead of feeling safe, relaxed, and devoted.

When a person is in low alert, they give up easily. This person puts up with situations, which otherwise could be changed because he is used to thinking that giving up is always the safest thing to do.

EXERCISE: FOR ALL RELATIVES

It seems very direct talking about private parts, but this is where you can feel how you are right now. In most cultures, we find it difficult to have a relaxed relationship to our genitals, and that is a part of the problem. Normally, we don't notice them, since they are connected to shame. However, our gut feeling works much better when our private parts are relaxed because that enables us to breathe deeper down our body, and to be attentive toward ourselves.

If you are a woman, close your eyes and try to sense the entrance to your vagina – and if you are a man, your perineum. Are you TOTALLY relaxed there, right now? Many high alert people almost never relax in this area. This naturally affects your sexuality, body posture and stress level.

If you want to work on it, you can do so a couple of times every day. Feel that place (I call it your anchor), and relax aaaaaaaaaaaltogether there, while you breathe deeply.

In the beginning, it feels awkward and doesn't make any difference, but when you do this exercise several times a day – maybe even once every hour; after all, it only takes 10 seconds – you will gradually start noticing a difference. Just sit, relax, close your eyes and let go of the tension in those muscles.

This will get you in touch with your body which in turn connects you to yourself, which is what is lost when you're with a narcissist. If you feel resistance towards doing this exercise, it just underlines how alienated you have become with your own body. Take it back!

You can't expect to be able to do this exercise if you are close to the narcissist – there your body needs to be on guard because you always instinctively feel threatened.

When we are ashamed or feel that we owe something, we feel that we are not good enough, and we tend to hide, physically and emotionally, when we feel inadequate.

One way of overcoming this is talking to another person about how YOU feel – a person, who can help you see that your feeling of inadequacy is just a bad story, which you are allowed to let go of, in order to give yourself space, happiness and calmness to live your own life.

NARCISSISTS AND LOGIC

If you have tried to confront a narcissist, you know you can forget everything about logical sense and good arguments. If you are on the same side, especially in the beginning of your acquaintance, you will be impressed by the narcissist's sharp, analytic abilities and his capability of taking on the whole world. But if you disobey the narcissist's rules, the world turns upside-down until you are unable to recognize it.

During discussions, the narcissist is the world champion when it comes to twisting the truth, turning your arguments against you, and making you doubt what you actually experience. Only if you have concrete physical evidence, the narcissist admits – and then, of course, he is not really to blame for the circumstances.

Narcissists gladly take the credit for something which you have done and seem totally astonished and almost insulted, when you point out this fact. Afterwards, when you seek justice, they accuse you of attention seeking. You learn that you can't insist on getting recognized for your results. This is because the narcissist perceives you as part of them and therefore feel naturally entitled to own your accomplishments.

At the same time, they are neither grateful nor happy for your effort. They will probably sulk and accuse you of being dominating, when you didn't ask for their advice. They might do so, even if you have asked them, whether they had an idea or wanted to take the initiative, and their answer was evasive.

#EXAMPLE

Betty wants to go on vacation with her boyfriend and his two children. When she asks him if he wants to, he replies: "It would be nice ..." Betty asks him where he wants to go, but he just shrugs his shoulders, and she starts planning a trip to Bulgaria. She asks him if he wants to go to Bulgaria, but he is almost silent, he just shrugs it off and says: "Why not?"

Betty arranges everything, and she is looking forward to the journey. It is obvious that her boyfriend doesn't care about it, and he seems quite reluctant when she tells him about Bulgaria and all the adventures ahead.

Several times, she asks him whether he is certain that he wants to go, and he halfheartedly confirms that.

During the vacation, he doesn't seem to care about getting out, and Betty almost has to drag them out to the attractions. The children fight constantly, and her boyfriend sulks. He just wants to sleep or watch Netflix, and Betty feels lonely. When they return home, she wants to talk about the vacation and her unredeemed expectations. Her boyfriend says that he finds her dominating, and that she doesn't let him relax.

When they visit some friends and are asked about the vacation, the boyfriend makes it sound like it was his idea, and that it was him who wanted to go to Bulgaria. In his description, the trip sounds like a magical experience. When they return home that night, Betty tries to start a dialogue about what is going on because she wants to understand, but her boyfriend just gets cross and accuses her of always wanting to take credit for everything.

DO YOU SAY WHAT YOU MEAN?

Are you saying yes, when you mean no? Regardless of the cause for this, you are violating yourself, when you say yes to something, which you don't really want to do. Whether this is caused by fear of reprisals, to avoid trouble, or to maintain peace and quiet in the house, the result is the same: Nothing changes, as long as you don't set boundaries for what you want to accept.

Your self-image must never be defined by how other people treat you. You are lovable, when YOU feel lovable – no matter what others do or how they act. Treat yourself lovingly, and that will define your self-image.

You will be accused of being unreasonable by the narcissist when you speak your truth and you can find comfort in the fact that what other people find unreasonable is because of how they perceive the world, it doesn't mean they have the right to define your truth. As long as you stay responsible for what goes on inside you and don't act mean like the narcissist, you're good.

Try to say no when you mean no, even though the narcissist convinces you to say yes instead - and he will do that - and write down how often this happens. How many times do you want to give up on yourself? Is that reasonable to you?

AM I THE NARCISSIST?

Because the narcissist projects – throws his own weak points over upon others – you might react strongly. When you experience that you react strongly, which is probably new to you, it is natural to assume that you might be the narcissist.

When you're with a narcissist and you examine the official criteria for narcissism and see your own actions, you will find examples that you actually DO display narcissistic behavior– and that is terrifying. You have to remember how you acted BEFORE you met the narcissist.

Did you display the same characteristics back then? Probably not. Do you display the same characteristics, when you are spending time with your closest friend? Probably not.

In other words, you have been "infected" – just like the mythic vampire makes a human a vampire by biting its throat and dripping a bit of vampire poison into the wound.

When you let go of the narcissist, you can work on getting back to a more suitable behavior, but it can be hard to do on your own. For this process, it is important to involve a network and other people who can support you, maybe even a therapist. Remember, the narcissist will never be in therapy, because they are always right, so the fact that you see what needs to change in your behaviour and you're willing to work with it, is proof that you're not a narcissist.

Besides, you are probably well aware that the narcissist rarely admits that something is the matter with him – and the fact that you are reading this book, is another sign that you do know that something in your behavior is unsuitable, and that you wish to do something about it.

We all have a shady side – deep, dark places inside us. Most people are ashamed of them, and they don't want to stand by them or openly admit that they exist. That is normal.

The more you open up; share your shady sides with others, accept them and contain them inside you; the stronger you are on your own, and the more resistant to people who want to manipulate you by pointing out your dark sides and giving you senses of shame and guilt, you will be.

#EXAMPLE

"You are so messy! There must be a lot of mess inside your head – a chaos of dimensions – which you don't show others, since you are THAT messy!" says the narcissist Tony to his girlfriend.

PJ, Tony's girlfriend, feels exposed, and she is ashamed and feels inadequate because she does have that chaos inside herself, just as Tony says. Pia feels that she has a lesser right to take up space in their relationship because of her mess, and she subconsciously makes herself smaller and insignificant by talking herself down: "No, that is unimportant. I'll just do without," she says, if there is only one slice of bread left in the fridge.

Insignificant, invisible, unimportant – this is what PJ has become during her two years in a relationship with Tony.

If PJ had stood up for her inner chaos, she could have said: "Yes, that's true. Sometimes there is chaos inside me. It isn't nice. Do you know the feeling of something inside you not being nice?" – and thereby inviting an open discussion about shady sides. In a relationship with a narcissist, that would probably be a dead-end, but in a sounder relationship, PJ would take ownership for what she contains. That would be a gift to the relationship and a possibility for exploring what hides inside all of us, together.

ARE YOU AFRAID THAT YOU ARE THE NARCISSIST?
WHEN ALL THE CLEVER PEOPLE TELL YOU THAT YOU
SHOULD STOP LISTENING TO
THE NARCISSIST'S CRITICISM, AND HE TELLS YOU THAT YOU
ARE THE NARCISSIST
BECAUSE YOU DON'T LISTEN TO CRITICISM?
WELL, YOU HAVE THIS BOOK IN YOUR HANDS.
THE FIRST STEP IS TO GET OUT OF THE RELATIONSHIP.
COMPLETELY!
THEN YOU HAVE TO WORK ON GETTING BACK TO YOURSELF
- TO THE PERSON YOU WERE,
BEFORE YOU MET THE NARCISSIST.
OR, IF YOU ARE THE CHILD OF A NARCISSIST, THEN FIND
THE PERSON, YOU REALLY ARE
- DOWN TO BASICS: THE BEST VERSION OF YOU.

LACK OF EMPATHY

Adult children of addicts and the mentally ill, including narcissists, may appear empathy-lacking because their survival strategy throughout childhood has been "not to sense and feel". When we don't sense ourselves, we are unable to sense others. Then, there is no empathy with ourselves, and consequently not with others. The difference between them and the narcissists is that the adult children are aware that something in their life is not quite right, and they often seek help and take responsibility for it.

The narcissist is incapable of showing true empathy toward others. He can't love, and he can't feel with other people – but he can fake it! The narcissist will call a therapist and claim that something is wrong with him, and that his loved ones suffer from it. "It must be my fault that he is so troubled. I just don't understand what I do wrong!"

If the therapist doesn't have the proper tools, he or she may "fall for the lie", and slowly, but steadily, becomes a team member on the narcissist's side, against the relative, who often really may appear hysterical, incoherent, confused, and self-contradictory.

In a relationship with a narcissist, no matter whether you are the partner or the child, there is only room for one person – and that is the narcissist. You have to compromise, you have to let go of your needs, your boundaries, and your wishes in order to make space for the narcissist.

In a love relationship, you will end up being invisible, and then the narcissist is unable to sense and feel himself; only his own dissatisfaction.

Consequently, he has to get rid of you like an old, smelly dishcloth, and he has to search for a new and fresh supply for his big, empty vessel of self-worth.

#EXAMPLE

Daniel's father is dissatisfied. Before Daniel visits him, his father says: "You rarely come over," and when Daniel is there, his father says: "You don't care about me," and then he spends the rest of the time bickering over everything between heaven and earth. He pities himself and hints that Daniel isn't good enough. No matter WHAT Daniel does, how HARD he tries, it is never quite enough. He is never truly able to satisfy his father.

Daniel's father talks about being alone, that people are selfish and preoccupied with themselves. Daniel's father never says that he is responsible for finding friends himself, or for being good company, so people like spending time with him. He just thinks that other people should do something. Daniel's father says that Daniel is the only one he has left, but also continues that Daniel probably doesn't care and is only concerned with himself.

Daniel protests and tells his father that he DOES care, to which the father replies that if that was true, Daniel would come around more often instead of being so self-absorbed. Daniel feels the knot in his stomach grow, when his father speaks like that, and something inside him struggles. At the same time, he gets angry with his father – and then he apologizes for his father's behavior. After all, he is just an old man, who is unable to figure out life.

Daniel never apologizes for himself – always his father. When Daniel gets angry with him, he feels guilty. There is not much understanding of Daniel and his feelings – neither from his father or from Daniel.

The lack of empathy is also evident, when you have sex with the narcissist. In an equal and loving relationship, sex is a reciprocal present full of presence and intimacy.

To the narcissist, sex is a commodity – something to trade, either to achieve something, to gain power, or to punish a victim. Sex can be a performance. Sex with true intimacy, including calmness and presence in a relationship, is difficult for a narcissist. The narcissist's partner might experience this as emotional abuse, when love becomes something you trade, or something you give or take away at a whim.

#EXAMPLE

Karen is in a relationship with Ian. Before they moved in together, they often went away on weekend getaways and adventure trips, and Karen fell completely for Ian's adventurous spirit and his "full- speed-ahead"-attitude.

However, many of those weekends went wrong. Often, Karen had a gut feeling that Ian got bored, if they hadn't made any plans. Besides, he would get cross, if Karen wanted to talk and cuddle after sex because "he couldn't cope with that right now". On the other side, Ian could be full of initiative and very seductive, and it was after a particularly steamy night that he suggested that they should move in together.

After a while, Karen realized that Ian struggled with finding peace and quiet in everyday life. Their life together varied between wild sex, where Karen almost had difficulty keeping up, and periods with no sex at all because Ian didn't feel like it. Besides, he claimed that he felt that she kept him under surveillance, when they had had some days without any activities or events.

ADULT CHILDREN OF NARCISSISTS

The expression "adult children" stems from the concept of Alcoholics Anonymous. Within Alcoholics Anonymous they talk about adult children in order to specify that this is adults, who were children in a particular situation. So far, this is the best definition that we have: That adult children are adults, who once were children during certain circumstances, for instance adult children of narcissistic parents or adult children of addicts. There are some common characteristics for that particular group of adults.

Adult children from narcissistic parents carry around guilt as big as the planet Earth. If you ask them what they are guilty of, or why they ought to feel ashamed, they find it very difficult to give a proper answer. They just have this indefinable sense of being guilty, being wrong, saying or doing the wrong thing – always.

As a consequence, many adult children from narcissists spend endless thoughts and words to explain and defend what they say and do – no matter whether it is necessary or not. Unfortunately, explanations and verbal defenses often make the person seem TRULY guilty. It corresponds to a situation, where $2 is missing. Nobody accuses you of having stolen the money, but still, you feel guilty and responsible and start explaining why it couldn't be you, who took them. It seems suspicious, and as if you are trying to hide your guilt.

Even when you have every reason to be angry – if someone lets you down, lies to you, or treats you badly – you are going to take responsibility in order to explain yourself, instead of just saying: "This is absolutely not ok!" and not make further explanations or defense speeches.

A narcissistic parent follows one of two patterns: Absorbed or overlooked.

Both patterns destroy the child's health, and it has profound consequences into adulthood.

Absorbed: The parent will absorb the child, and the child is expected to be a parent to the adult – to take responsibility for the parent's feelings and wellbeing, to believe the same as the parent, to support and defend the adult in everything. The child fails to develop its own personality but grows into a clone of the parent. It becomes a lifelong task to figure out who he or she is, to learn to set boundaries, to understand that fairness is subjective, and to realize that the adult child has every right to exist in this world with its own personality; even when others disapprove or fail to recognize it.

Overlooked: The child lacks sincere interest and true presence from the parent, who will indicate that there is something the child can do in order to receive contact, love, and presence, but that will never happen. This sows a seed within the child, which might make the child change between fighting like a warrior to being good enough, clever enough, proper enough – and being resigned, full of stress, and energy-lacking – for the rest of its life. The adult child will feel left out without even being it, and it will struggle to feel that it belongs in this world.

#EXAMPLE

Mariah, 22 years. Mariah has no friends. There is no one who wants to spend time with her. She is self-absorbed, egotistic, loud speaking, self-promoting, empathy-lacking, bragging, and a know-it-all.

Mariah believes that "clever" is the right thing to be, and she fails to understand that others don't think that she is extremely cool. Men are frightened of her because she is mannish, is a loudmouth; and she drinks, swears and smokes like a dock worker. The men, who manage to get close to her, are either like her father, or they just want to sleep with her and nothing more.

Her only role model was her father because her mother was an alcoholic and didn't speak 100 coherent words to her throughout her childhood. Mariah lies because her truth compass is turned upside down, just like her father's, and she is able to conjure the craziest lies and even believing them with only a tiny hint of bad conscience inside her heart, which she has never learned to listen to. She feels lonely, but she doesn't understand that she holds the key to do something about it.

Her father has told her that she is someone special. Better than others. But not as good as him. And never good enough. It is difficult to navigate socially, when you know that you can never be good enough and at the same time have to believe that you are better than others. There is no other way than becoming a clone of her father.

When Mariah is 24 years old, she finally meets a person, who is brave enough to tell her directly that she takes up too much space, and that she needs to revise her moral compass – and that message hurts her enough to make her realize that she has to change something in order to stop the pain.

#EXAMPLE

Charlotte is 15 years old and wishes to study history but especially her mother speaks against it, for "that education is useless!" Her parents, Inge and Ebbe, try to persuade her to study other subjects, which they are more capable of understanding.

Inge and Ebbe disapprove of many of Charlotte's friends because they lead another kind of life or have different opinions from what they wish for Charlotte, and her parents mock her friends and tell Charlotte that "they are not good for you".

When Charlotte enters high school, she develops exam fear because she feels that she has to prove her worth, and when she starts university, it has become so heavy that she finds a psychologist and enters a group for people with exam fear. When she tells her mother about it, her mother laughs and says that only weak people seek a psychologist and that it doesn't make anything better.

Emotional Incest

This is a rather controversial concept because many people, who have been subjected to incest, feels that this phrasing and connection devalues the word 'incest'. However, there is no better word for it because this is exactly what happens to a child growing up with a narcissistic parent.

Like the adult in an incest situation uses the child to satisfy his or her own sexual needs, the narcissistic parent uses the child to satisfy his or her emotional needs.

Incest is not only sexual and physical. When a child is subjected to sexual incest, the child is at the same time subjected to emotional incest, but we now know that the emotional incest often stands alone.

When the adult expects the child to cover the adult's emotional needs and to take on an adult's role in the relationship to the parent, it is called emotional or psychological incest.

Emotional incest is just as damaging to the child as physical incest. The child brings violent and life- transforming consequences into adulthood.

For instance, there is no room for the child's own needs, which means that the child grows up into a human being unable to feel its own needs because those needs always have been suppressed, made insignificant, or even unwelcome.

The adult's needs have taken up so much space that the child has learned that its own needs are unimportant, and that it first and foremost is responsible for covering other peoples' needs.

Besides, it is never acceptable to say no, to back out, or to set boundaries in that kind of family. Not that children would ever say no to their parents – it happens rarely in families with emotional incest, but they say no with their body language and their attitude. The children show that they don't feel like doing what is expected from them. They signal that this is not nice for them. Often with subtle body language, which sound adults can and will read – and respect.

In a family with emotional incest the child is neither seen nor respected. To the psychologically incestuous parent his or her own problems take up so much space that there isn't room for or mental energy to read and respect the child's boundaries.

PUT YOUR FINGER DOWN INTO A BLENDER AND TRY TO EXPLAIN THE BLENDER THAT IT MUSTN'T HURT YOU. THAT MAKES JUST AS MUCH SENSE AS WHEN YOU TRY TO EXPLAIN TO THE NARCISSIST THAT HE MUSTN'T HURT YOU. INSTEAD, YOU MIGHT REFRAIN FROM PUTTING YOUR FINGER INTO THE BLENDER?!

As a consequence, the child grows up and turns into an adult, who finds it difficult to say no and set boundaries. In combination with the lacking ability to feel itself, we have a grown-up person, who rarely or never sets boundaries or demands; who is unable to feel what he or he wants or doesn't want to do; and who lives for meeting other peoples' needs before its own, when it comes to relations with other adults.

At the same time, the person's needs are never met, and therefore he or he will constantly try to get them fulfilled from others. The person has learned that "I must not meet my own demands, only others' needs", so he is unable to fulfill his own emotional needs and constantly has to search his close relations for satisfaction.

The adult child has been programmed into thinking that "my needs are insignificant, and I can't expect to get them fulfilled." It leads to seeking relations, where the adult child will meet another person's demands, but rarely has his own satisfied. Thereby, the adult child becomes the perfect, but unhappy helper.

When these people have children, they often continue that tradition of emotional incest since there simply aren't enough reserves to be a proper parent with strength and overview – where should they get that from? Who should have taught them?

Emotional incest happens in many families but regrettably, it is a typical consequence for the children in a family where one of the parents suffered from chronic illness – physical, mental or both. Unfortunately, it is ALWAYS a consequence in narcissistic families.

Here are two examples from different types of families in order to give you some perspective. If you grew up in a narcissistic family, you probably recognize the children's experiences.

#EXAMPLE

Elsa narrates: "My father was depressed, and for long periods at the time he was lying in bed, crying, and he had an unhappy expression. We were told to sneak quietly around because he was overly sensitive to noises, and he needed to sleep. I wasn't allowed to bring home friends, and I wasn't allowed to visit them either because my father needed me.

Often, I sat on his bedside, held his hand and comforted him. I told him that everything would be all right. He told me that I was the only one who understood him and cared for him. When I tried to say that so did my mother, he just turned his head away. He obviously thought that I was the only one who took his illness seriously.

It became a way of living. My father always came first; it was more important for me to take care of him than playing with my friends. After all, he couldn't help it. My mother often got angry with me and scolded me for not doing my homework, when I grew older, but it was more important to look after my father.

I think, maybe, my mother was a bit jealous of our close relationship. My father and I could talk about everything when I sat by his bed. Or, he did. I didn't have much to tell aside from what I did at school.

When he sometimes felt well, I spent much of my time making him happy and keeping him happy, so he wouldn't become depressed again."

As an adult, Elsa didn't think at first that she had suffered privations – on the contrary. She felt that she had had a close relationship with her father and that she had played an important part in the family as a nursing aide and someone who kept everybody happy.

Not until her late twenties, Elsa started feeling that something was wrong. She never knew what she wanted to do. She couldn't back out when someone crossed her boundaries because she just wanted to make other people happy. A few years before, Elsa had had a breakdown with stress because she had never learned to take care of herself. She kept falling for demanding and unstable men. She started therapy because she was stressed again and afraid of falling into depression and ending up being chronically ill just like her father.

#EXAMPLE

Line is another and very relevant example. She narrates about her father, who was an alcoholic with clear narcissistic characteristics:

"My mother and I never knew which mood my father would be in, when he came home. Sometimes he arrived in an excellent mood, and then you just had to be as well in order not to destroy it and create a bad atmosphere at home. Our family must have looked like the dancing scene in Snow White, when it was like that. Everything bad was blown away, and we laughed and had fun. If anyone dared being in a bad mood on such a day – and in our teenage years, it could be myself or my brother – we were told that we sabotaged the brilliant atmosphere.

If my father was in a bad mood, when he came home, the same rules applied. We were walking on eggshells and watched our words because he flew off the handle over the slightest thing or broke down in tears, sitting on the kitchen floor claiming that nobody liked him. Then we all had to comfort him.

Once, my brother tried to tell him that HE was sabotaging the brilliant atmosphere, just to try to let him taste his own medicine, but he just cried even more and told him that he was right. He said that he was a lousy father, and that we were probably better off without him.

If he arrived home late, we could, after all, be almost certain that he was drunk, and then we just had to lead him into the living room, where he would fall asleep on the sofa.

When I became a teenager, I felt that I had to meet my boyfriends in secret because my father would be so rude toward them. He thought that he was funny, but he was demeaning and nasty. It was as if no boy was good enough or rich enough for me.

When I moved in with a man for the first time, I felt guilty because I knew that my father would miss me when he was feeling down."

Line joined therapy because her husband had suffered a severe and long depression, and she felt worn down, but didn't think that she could leave him. It was a difficult dilemma.

Line hadn't discovered that she always was "the one who took care of everyone" at the cost of herself, and it was a sudden awakening.

THE TABOO

Emotional incest is far more common than we are aware of. There are two reasons why we fail to address it.

The first is that it is embarrassing to have been a victim – we are struck by the same kind of shame and tabooing as victims of sexual incest. Even though it stands clear for everybody that the child is not to blame and doesn't have to feel shameful, most incest victims own the blame and fight against it for years.

The question "Couldn't you just have said no?" releases a hurricane of guilt that the obvious thing to do wasn't at all obvious, while you stood in the middle of it. And where could you have learned? Often, the partner of the incestuous person is a really good facilitator, who either knows what is going on but shuts their eyes, or who doesn't realize what is happening.

When the child from the example above sits by her father's bedside that often, her mother knows that it is wrong, but instead of facing the discussion with her husband, she gets angry with the child. She doesn't stop her husband from clinging to their child – maybe because she has no idea what to do about it. The mother doesn't feel that she has any alternative, and therefore she keeps her mouth shut.

However, that doesn't excuse her for not taking responsibility. The taboo is nourished by the mother's behavior because the family never speaks openly about what is going on.

WHEN NOBODY INTERVENES

The other reason is doubt. Since it is rare that someone intervenes, the adult child often doubts that the feeling of something being wrong is true at all. "When nobody calls out for action, makes objections, or protests, I may be totally wrong about this."

It can be difficult to hold on to yourself because many of the children, who have experienced emotional incest, often are met with difficult and illogical questions, when they try to talk about their experiences.

Besides, many who try to open up about it are confronted with questions like: "But did they hit you?" or "Were you sexually abused?" – and if you answer no to these questions, the person then easily concludes that "it can't have been that difficult, then."

For instance, Elsa was often met with the question: "But were you forced to sit by your father's bed?"

No, she wasn't. She chose that herself, but if she had been able to feel that she was free to do something else, for instance spending time on her own or with friends, she probably would have done so.

Another important angle to intervention is that the child's unconditional loyalty will cause the child to protest if someone tries to intervene. In a concrete situation, the parent will call on the child's loyalty as a defense, and the child has no possibility to escape that.

#EXAMPLE

"She is Daddy's girl. She thinks what her father thinks!" says the father smilingly and looks at little Rhonda with eyes lurking as deep in the abyss as an empty universe.

Rhonda knows that she has to nod. But her father's new friend, Corinne, protests: "Ahh, you can't just conclude this without knowing if she really DOES agree? I gather that she is allowed to think for herself?"

Father doesn't look at Corinne. He looks at Rhonda, and in his eyes she sees the black inside him, it peeks out, and her stomach churns. Now the world gets dangerous. She has to make peace. "No," she says.

"I agree with Dad. And I have thought about it myself."

Rhonda is 9 years old, and she knows that she is responsible for the good atmosphere.

Both private people or professionals have asked me, whether forced removal from home is a solution, but I don't believe that.

How tough it may sound the child will not experience forceful removal as an appropriate solution. On the contrary, the child will see the new adults as opponents in a bitter war against the family's integrity, and the child will feel guilty because it is no longer close to the parent and able to take responsibility for the emotions, the atmosphere, and the discomfort.

CRITERIA FOR EMOTIONAL INCEST

Below you will find some criteria for when you have been subjected to emotional incest. Patricia Love has discussed them in her book "The Emotional Incest Syndrome: What to Do When a Parent's Love Rules Your Life", which is specifically about emotional incest.

Patricia Love gives many good examples of how a parent can invade the child's emotional life by either choosing the child as someone special or by blaming it for the family's accidents.

Try and determine, if your upbringing fits any of these points. If you can agree to three or more of these points, you have to some degree or another been subjected to emotional incest.

1. I was the source of emotional support for one of my parents.

2. I understood that my parents didn't want me to marry or move too far away from home.

3. My boyfriends / girlfriends were never good enough for one or both of my parents.

4. I felt that I had to withhold my own needs in order to protect my parent(s).

5. I felt partly or wholly responsible for my parents' happiness.

6. Sometimes I felt invaded by a parent.

7. My parent had unrealistic expectations for my achievements.

8. My parent was preoccupied with addiction, work, or other interests instead of me.

9. My parent behaved as and considered himself/herself my best friend.

The loyalty within incestuous families becomes a problem later in life too. The child is brought up to keep the secret instead of taking itself seriously and being authentic, for instance with sentences like: "This is our little secret." – "This stays between us, nobody else would understand." – "We are something special, you and I."

These words, which on the surface seem innocent, create an understanding within the child that without the alliance with the parent, the child is lost, and it will never be understood or welcomed in the rest of the world.

EXERCISE: WHAT MAKES YOU HAPPY?

When you are working on this, the starting point is imagining yourself in concrete situations, where you are the most loving and sound parent for yourself, and then ask: "What would be good for me right now?" Often the answer is unknown because you never have learned to feel and acknowledge what is good for you.

Make a list of things that make you happy and calm. When you get to know yourself better, the list might grow, and then you can look at it every time you find yourself in an uncomfortable situation.

You will probably feel guilty when you begin doing something good for yourself, but it will soon become easier. When you become better at doing good things for you, taking care of yourself, and taking care of you, you will discover an added bonus: It will be much easier for you to feel whether the things you are doing for others make you happy or exhausted – and then you will be able to do other good things for others, which also make you happy.

Besides, you can decide that you never again want to keep toxic secrets, and in that way, you can stop the unsound loyalty.

#EXAMPLE

Mark grew up with a narcissistic father and an alcoholic mother. At home, loyalty was an absolute demand. He was supposed to smile and be happy on the surface, so other adults could see that his parents were good parents. He was responsible for their acknowledgment. His father was a famous singer and Mark knew he would never be the most important thing in his life.

In his thirties, Mark was tormented by all the secrets, and he made a conscious choice to openly discuss what had happened during his upbringing. When his father committed suicide, the media contacted him, and he was faced with a difficult choice between loyalty and honesty. He chose honesty – about his parents, himself and the consequences, which had been his companion into adulthood. His openness enabled him to let go of the shame and to choose himself and do what he wished with his life.

It became obvious that most of the consequences were pretty easy to discard, when he didn't try to hide or deny the truth. And it actually is like that. When we put the difficult things into words and share them, they shrink, and over time they become insignificant.

The narcissist parent is characterized by:

- disrespecting your boundaries
- asking without giving you a chance for an honest reply
- competing with you, the child, on uneven conditions
- lying about you, to you, for you
- controlling you
- manipulating you
- brainwashing you into seeing the world from the parent's perspective
- diminishing you and ridiculing you

As an adult child of narcissistic parents, you will throughout your life – or until you do something about it – have problems when it comes to:

- setting boundaries
- sensing yourself
- sticking to what is right for you
- not making you and your needs invisible in relationships
- being co-dependent on partners and friends and/or never letting others get too close to you
- being very, very, very self-critical
- feeling chronic guilt and shame
- feeling empty
- lacking confidence in yourself and others
- suffering from anxiety and depression
- behaving in a pleasing manner

#EXAMPLE

Charlotte felt guilty when she had to explain to others why the situation with her parents was so serious that she had to break with them, and she felt alone. Even though she had her boyfriend, her parents-in-law, and her grandparents, she missed the contact with her parents; no matter how damaging it was.

She felt abandoned. She was orphaned when she was 23, but her parents were still alive, and she felt that she had to defend her situation. Still, she knew that she would feel even more lonely if she submitted to her parents' family structure.

How Do I Live With A Narcissist?

Sometimes you realize that it is necessary to let the narcissist stay in your life for emotional or practical reasons. If the narcissist is a daughter, sister, or mother, it might be difficult and will have huge consequences for the rest of the family, if you decide to cut off the contact entirely. Or, it can be in the workplace, and where you like your job, but have to cooperate with or work for a narcissist.

Even though you long for shipping the narcissist off to a desert island, where she is unable to harm you or others, you sometimes have to accept that the narcissist is a part of your life.

If it is a superior or a parent, you as an adult can try to minimize contact. It might work when it comes to parents, who are old and infirm, and maybe live in a nursing home, but rarely when it comes to a superior. You have to make a choice: My mental health or the job.

For this reason, these tools can help you.

The most efficient way to deal with a narcissist is staying emotionally detached. This means that under no circumstances should you allow yourself to get hurt, carried away, angry, disappointed, annoyed or in any other way affected by the narcissist's statements and actions. This method is called "Grey Rock" because your facial expression and your mind must remain unaffected.

If you throw a stick in the water, the water moves and adapts to the stick. If you throw a stick upon frozen water – ice – nothing happens, and that is what you have to work with when the narcissist is going to stay in your life. Your facial expression and your body language must become steady as ice, so nothing happens, when the narcissist throws his drama-stick at you.

There is a "but", and that is if the narcissist is a close relation like a parent or partner, you might risk that your emotional detachment affects you too, meaning that you become unaware of when you are getting hurt or angry, and that you end up neglecting to take care of yourself in these situations.

Another way to manage narcissists in your life is through humor and laughter. Not sarcasms, since narcissists are completely incapable of handling that – even though they generously use it themselves.

For instance, you can fend off a demeaning tone of voice or words with: "Hey, you are certainly not beating around the bush, are you?" – and then laugh gently, as you would do with a child who said a swear word or something inappropriate. You know that the child would use that word against you or shut down and go into itself, if you had scolded it, and sometimes bad behavior simply can't be ignored.

While he was alive, I experienced this with my father a couple of times – that I could make jokes about him, when he was rude, and it ALMOST made him apologize, but it certainly made him stop being abominable, made him silent, or changed his focus.

Therapists often use an expression called "tag-along". This is a way for handling something difficult, for instance an unpleasant sensation or a resistance, and that is kind of what happens.

Below are a few examples of how to deal with narcissists, whom you are unable to get rid of. And no, I am not going to give you a recipe for staying in a relationship with a narcissist because I wouldn't wish that upon my worst enemy. It is damaging to your health, and it will slowly drive you to insanity and probably physically ill. You can end up with borderline, bi-polar disorder or narcissistic traits if you are close to a narcissist for too long.

Narcissists don't love, even though in glimpses it may seem so. It is a façade, a learned ability they use to capture their victims. Forget everything about changing them, curing them, or nurturing their positive sides. If the narcissist does not VOLUNTARILY, LOUD AND CLEAR, directly say: "Something is wrong with me, and I want to do something about it, and I am going to seek help," there is nothing you can do, and you just have to get away as quickly as possible. These examples are about relations, which are necessary in order to function in a family or in the workplace.

#EXAMPLE

My father, Poul, who was an actor, could – out of the blue, and without any warning or cause – get beastly with a vengeance toward his girlfriend, whoever she was at the time.

He would say things such as:

"Yes, with that hair I truly understand that your parents decided not to have more children."

"I don't want you to come along, for others will pay more attention to your nose than to me on the stage."

"Well, you're not the cleverest person, are you?"

"Your parents are so boring that you could mistake them for the wallpaper."

Usually, he would kind of smile. To those who knew him, it looked more like a sneer than a smile, and therefore, if someone became offended, he could say: "Obviously you have no sense of humor, either," or: "Well, the rest of Denmark understands my kind of humor, but you don't. It is no wonder that I sometimes feel lonely."

If the girlfriend insisted, he would just maintain that it was a joke, but he regularly repeated his insults, and she would never doubt that behind his "humor", he found her ugly, stupid, boring and useless, and that she was supposed to feel grateful because he bothered spending more time and energy on her.

Sometimes, I could be lucky, when I experienced him like that, and by "tagging along", I could shut him down, so he stopped or did a U-turn.

"I am happy that you mention her nose, for with your floppy ears, you two are a perfect match."

"Yes, it is absolutely the hair that determines whether a person is worth loving," and then I would copy him: With a light grin and a sparkling eye, I would shoot my verbal arrow and stop him.

In my family, I became the savior, and I became excellent at warding off attacks on others; to fight for the innocent and comfort his girlfriends when they were unhappy about his abusive behavior. In that way, we lived in the drama triangle with which all families with dysfunctional patterns live – not only families with narcissists. In dysfunctional families, there often is an offender (here the narcissist), a victim (the target), and a savior (the one trying to ease the situation).

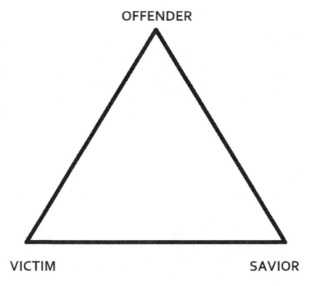

OFFENDER

VICTIM   SAVIOR

*In the book **"Your Hero's Journey – How to get rid of negative side effects from your childhood"** by Mariah Wolfe and Charlotte Lindhardt, the drama triangle is thoroughly explained.*

When you try to fend off the narcissist's drama and take part in the drama triangle, it feels like you are sly and narcissistic. You may feel guilty and shameful because you are no better than the narcissist. This is a natural reaction. When you are out of reach from the narcissist's clutches, you can return to a healthier behavior.

#EXAMPLE

Heather has two sons with a narcissistic man, whom she has left, but she fears what he might do in the future. She wants to know how she can prepare and predict what is going to happen in order to lessen the consequences. When I speak with her, I say:

"You have been through the worst! The narcissist makes you feel that you have to know every little corner of your life and mind, so you are able to predict your own reaction; otherwise he will be able to strike at any given point.

Be concrete. What will he be able to do?! If you don't know, then close your eyes, breathe, and try to imagine it. Again: You HAVE been through the worst, and you got away, so he can never do anything worse than what you have already experienced!"

I clarify it: "You can imagine anything, but this is where you ask yourself whether it is realistic at all that anybody will believe the narcissist.

If he wants to gossip about you being mentally ill, or he wants to doubt your credibility, you must ask yourself, WHO the narcissist can tell, who is going to believe him instead of you. Think about it and be concrete.

The power of the narcissist is that we NEVER know what to expect. The insecurity toward them makes us very attentive toward THEIR actions and moods; and that is part of their power.

We have to break free and turn to look at ourselves instead of being focused on them. They CAN do something which hurts us, but if we have to live "on guard" all the time, we don't live – and that will wear on our physical and mental health."

Heather thinks about it and says that the worst thing her ex could do was to say to people at her children's school that she committed incest. I remind her that her boys are 13 and 16 years old, and they don't want any contact with their father, so what would he gain by that? It is an awful and terrible scenario, and I calm her down by saying that his only aim is getting attention from her and putting himself in a favorable light:

"If you panic and start defending yourself and appear frightened, he wins. On the other hand, if you remain calm and just say, "What a load of nonsense" and shrug your shoulders, his power over you diminishes, and gradually, as he finds out that you don't react, he will stop trying and turn his attention toward another victim. Even though it is awful to wish that, it is better than you suffer from his actions – you HAVE DONE your time with him."

The thought about the narcissist finding another victim than her seems to both calm and terrify her. He is relieved that it isn't going to be her, but she pities the next one. I tell that there is nothing she can do to save the next one but that there is a way:

"Don't get any bright ideas about saving the new victim. You already know that she wouldn't believe you, as you distrusted those who warned you in the beginning. You defended him by saying that they didn't understand him the way you do. It will be a waste of time warning her at that stage. If she is going to need your advice, she will seek you out

herself."

And it happens. I am aware of several examples where exes have created a network which is ready to take care of new victim-partners, and where they without any hidden agenda support her in realizing that the experience actually happened.

WHEN YOU GET OUT OF A RELATIONSHIP WITH A NARCISSISTIC PERSON,
YOU MIGHT BE PREOCCUPIED WITH THE NARCISSIST'S NEW RELATIONS,
AND YOU WILL BE FRUSTRATED THAT THEY SEEM IN LOVE OR HAPPY.
YOU MIGHT ALWAYS FEEL JEALOUS THAT THE NEW CHOSEN ONE APPARENTLY SEEMS TO GET EVERYTHING YOU DREAMT OF.
BUT THAT IS NOT THE CASE.
THE NARCISSIST IS UNABLE TO PROVIDE TRUE LOVE.
AT THE SAME TIME, YOU MUST KNOW THAT THE BEST SIGN OF YOUR HEALING FROM THE EXPERIENCE IS
THAT YOU ARE TOTALLY INDIFFERENT AS TO WHAT THE NARCISSIST IS DOING, WHO HE SPENDS TIME WITH, OR HOW THEY ARE FEELING!

#EXAMPLE

Tom and his son Chris are both narcissists. Tom is divorced from Chris's mother, Bonnie. Chris is an only child, and he alternately lives with his mother and father.

Hank and the rest of the family wish to have a close-knit family but are challenged because father and son are unable to distinguish moral values from whatever benefits those two. Sometimes father and son clash, and then the son stays with Bonnie or other family members for a few days, until the tempers cool down.

It is difficult to navigate within – including the different stories, which they tell the rest of the family. Some are true, some are their own version of the truth.

Some family members know that the two are narcissistic, but they don't want to go no contact. They know that the family peace disappears, if they do, and since it is a big family where only those two family members have unsound behavioral patterns, the others choose to live with it.

The rest of the family knows that any information from Tom and Chris must be checked or taken with a grain of salt.

For example, Tom tries to play off family members against each other, and instead of accepting the gossip as true, the family members talk to one another.

It is a classic attempt at triangulation, and since everybody talks with one another, it has no effect.

When Tom and Chris create a drama and try to involve the rest of the family, the strategy is to defuse the bomb and move focus.

For instance, when the son, Chris, lives with other family members, they consider it a welcome visit and not a necessity because of a mentally unstable father, and they talk about it in that way: "It's so good having you here. Now we have the chance to do something together," and if Chris starts bickering about his father, they say: "Yes, it can be a bit difficult but on the other hand it is really great that you want to visit us. Everybody needs some space from time to time." They talk the drama away and remove focus from it.

It might be clever using the same methods as the narcissists do. You just have to be aware that this is what you are doing, so it doesn't become a habit and a part of your personality.

#EXAMPLE

Bitten is at a family party, and during the evening she stands close to her brother-in-law, Christian. The brother-in-law has been part of the family for a few years, and he has been informed about Bitten's narcissistic tendencies, and after a couple of unpleasant episodes with Bitten, others have helped him to gently, but firmly, keep a distance from Bitten.

Bitten smiles confidentially at Christian and says: "I am sorry that you and I are not as close as we used to be. You don't really confide in me anymore. Is there any reason for that?"

Christian knows that the truth will cause trouble, and instead he acts surprised and says: "No, really? We are family. Of course, we are close. There is just not much to tell. You know, in the summer, the horses almost take care of themselves, and then we just go to work – and you know all about that anyway. It's just our quiet life and daily routines."

Christian has stopped confiding in Bitten, and he moves focus, whenever Bitten tries to confide in him.

Christian only talks about everyday occurrences like TV-shows and the weather so nothing can be twisted or turned and used against him.

If Christian told Bitten outright that he had stopped confiding in her because everything gets twisted and turned, Bitten would probably use exactly that method, and he wouldn't be able to recognize his own behavior at all, and thus she would create insecurity.

No matter whether you choose one strategy or the other, it is always tough to have a narcissistic relation. There is always a price to pay, and there will always be consequences. Therefore, you have to decide whether or not it is worth it. If you are unable to "get away", you have to keep the contact to a minimum.

Co-Parenting With A Narcissist

Ending a relationship with a partner often triggers off sorrow and emptiness. When we enter into a relationship, most people hope that it is for life.

It can be twice as painful whenever children are involved, and we have to share the parenting and make it work without taking the children as hostages.

When the other parent is a narcissistic person, it is even more painful, for as a starting point, the narcissist is unable to cooperate. He will always exploit, abuse, cross boundaries, change the deal, use guilt and rejection, humiliation, and manipulation.

This means that you as a parent have to take some precautions in order to survive the co-parenting; and that is just one side of it because there are also your children, who WILL become affected by the narcissist. Below are the most frequently asked questions from parents with joint custody, as well as my answers.

HOW DO I SPEAK TO MY CHILD ABOUT THE OTHER PARENT?

As a starting point, you don't talk about the other parent at all. The most important reason for this is that the narcissist is going to demand 100 % loyalty from your child, and if you say anything negative about the narcissist to the child or in the presence of the child, it will create a huge conflict within the child – and in the long run the child may withdraw from you.

Children always cooperate – not as we want, but as they subconsciously think is best – and they often support the weakest parent. Even though you were the narcissist's victim, you are not the weakest part - the narcissist is. A narcissist isn't well-balanced, is unable to manage relations, and lacks self-insight, and the child sees that.

If the other parent does something inappropriate toward you, you can share it with a friend at a time, when the child is out of hearing range.

#EXAMPLE

Little Mary is with her mother and asks her, "Why does Dad lie sometimes?" and Mary's mother answers like this: "Oh I am sorry you experience that. It must be very unpleasant to be lied to. It must also be confusing for you. I am so glad you are here and I will not lie to you. Hey, let's go for a walk and see if we can find some butterflies!"

Nothing is said about the narcissistic parent, but the child is heard and met with compassion and then the focus is changed.

WHY DOES MY CHILD REACT AGGRESSIVELY AFTER PARENTING TIME?

Many parents with joint custody experience a very violent reaction from their children, when they return after parenting time with the narcissistic parent.

Up to three days after the visit, the child can react aggressively and use words and expressions which would make a sailor blush. Regrettably, this is a common reaction. At the narcissist's home, the child experiences that it is not allowed to set boundaries; that it has to stay invisible, and that it is abused, and both verbally and emotionally rejected – and maybe even physically.

The child is unable to react at the narcissistic parent's home. It is neither possible nor allowed. Therefore, the child reacts where it feels safe – with you. It will be good to set it into words, but remember not to talk about the other parent; only about the child's reaction:

"Phew, sometimes, when we experience something really unpleasant, we want to be unpleasant ourselves. I truly understand that."

"You react because something inside you hurts. I understand that."

"I wish that I could make sure that it always was nice to be you."

Make sure to use short sentences full of understanding. You can set boundaries for what you want to put up with. Just don't do it in the same sentence as when you tell the child that you understand it because that will neutralize the effect of the compassion, which you wish to show the child. When you set boundaries, don't wait until you get angry. Put an end to it, while you still are able to do so firmly and lovingly.

"I don't want to fight. It hurts me. You are most welcome to go into your room and hit your duvet." If necessary, you can go too, and show how. Hit the duvet, perhaps with an angry shout – it is a great way to let out steam. Or, you can say:

"Hey, I don't like getting hit. How about we tickle each other or play tag instead of fighting?"

When you offer fun and other alternatives to unsound behavior the child learns to move focus, and that there are other ways to act out your anger. It is best if you participate in the activities since the child needs your intimacy and time together.

WHAT IS THE MOST IMPORTANT THING, WHICH I CAN DO FOR MY CHILD?

The most important thing you can do – and not just you, but all parents whether they have children with a narcissist or not – is to ensure that you have a good life surrounded by wonderful people; a life filled with laughter, healthiness and exercise, intimacy, sound boundaries and good relations.

When you have those things and are happy, you are the best role model for your child when it comes to showing how to live a fulfilled life, and you provide the child with a sanctuary where it is able to grow and be itself. Sometimes, I hear people arguing against divorce because they think it is better for a child to have two parents, but that is a bad argument.

The most important thing for a child is happy parents; so, if you are unhappy with your life, you need to make a better choice as a parent. The best thing you can do for your children is have an amazing life – whether single or in a relationship.

WHAT DO I DO WHEN THE CHILD TELLS ME ABOUT THE OTHER PARENT'S INAPPROPRIATE BEHAVIOR?

YOU TALK ABOUT THE CHILD, NOT ABOUT THE OTHER PARENT!

#EXAMPLE

Stefan comes home and says that he feels like his father doesn't really care about him. When he is with his father, Stefan often just sits with his laptop or watches TV, and his father is occupied with other things. Stefan's mother knows that she is supposed to talk about Stefan and not his father and says: "Urrgh. It is tough when it feels like another person doesn't really care. You don't deserve that. It is a difficult feeling to handle, and you should know that I care for you. You are a wonderful boy, and I feel lucky, when I spend time with you. How about a trip to the park?"

Stefan's mother talks about and recognizes Stefan's feelings, and she meets him where he is emotionally. She shows him understanding and that things are different at her place. Then she turns her attention toward something positive. She knows that he likes walking in the park, and she wants to encourage his positiveness.

It may be tempting to offer your children candy or cake as a consolation but comforting with unhealthy food is never a good solution. It is much better to offer an outdoor activity so the child – and you – get some exercise together. It creates a bond between you and activates energy and mental strength within you. The strategies you implement in your life with your child will be what they resort to when they grow up and have to handle difficult situations and emotions.

#EXAMPLE

Gitte tells her mother that her father called her a little whore. They are having dinner together, and Gitte doesn't look at her mother, but looks down at the table, and she says it casually. This signals that the child feels shameful, and therefore it is important to tread carefully.

Her mother says: "Ugh, that wasn't nice. Sometimes angry people can call others something, which feels really awful. That isn't ok. No matter what your father got angry about; he shouldn't call you something that unpleasant."

She pushes her chair away from the table, and with her hand, she shows Gitte that she can sit on her lap. She does, and she holds her and rocks her. She cries a little, and she strokes her hair. There is no reason to say anything else. It is more important to offer the child intimacy, a safe haven, and a place to contemplate the episode.

If the child comes home and asks: "What am I supposed to say to my father when he does or says something unpleasant?" you can say: "If I was you, I would go into my room and take a break. If it doesn't stop, you can call me or your granddad (or another resourceful person) and ask us to come and get you."

The reason for mentioning another resourceful person is that, due to the conflict of loyalty, sometimes it is safer for the child to contact another person rather than you. However, even with a grandparent, the narcissistic parent can say things such as: "Oh, you just run away, you don't care about me."

There are many ways to put the events into words, and it may help you to find a person like a therapist, a friend or another confidant; who can help you formulate concrete sentences. Abstain from feeling sorry for your child. It doesn't help your child that you pity it. Things are as they are, and it is better that you focus on creating joy, peace, and presence.

Besides, there are other things you can do as a parent with joint custody.

Keep the contact to a minimum. It goes for both the contact to the other parent in general, and for situations where you meet face to face, for instance when the child moves from place to place, at meetings, family gatherings etc. Avoid meetings, unless it is necessary.

When you are obliged to have contact with the other parent, make sure to keep a neutral tone of voice. Avoid emotionally charged feelings and words. Keep the communication at the same level as if you would with a business relation – short, concise and without feelings.

Set firm boundaries and make clear agreements with all institutions and parties involved with the child. You never know where the narcissist is going to react inappropriately, but you can set boundaries and make agreements, as soon as you discover where the other party's behavior becomes a problem.

For instance, if you have agreed that the other parent picks up the child from the school or kindergarten on Friday for parenting time during the weekend, you can agree – and always in writing through for example an email – with the parent and the institution at what time the picking up takes place. Then you and the institution can arrange that they contact you, if the child isn't picked up.

Remember that the narcissist will try to break boundaries, agreements, and promises to get you to react, so you need to have everything in writing. When you have made an agreement, you can send an e-mail with a confirmation, i.e.: "Hi John. We have agreed that you pick up Harold between 1 and 3 p.m. on Fridays on even weeks. If something else comes up, contact me before 1 p.m., then I'll pick him up."

It will probably be more difficult to plan your life because the narcissist will break agreements and try to hinder your living your own life. Tell people around you so they know that you might have to cancel or change plans at the last minute.

Support your child in developing its own personality, needs, and opinions. The narcissistic parent doesn't look upon the child as an independent individual with feelings and needs that must be nurtured and met. Instead, the child becomes an extension of the narcissist.

The narcissistic parent sees normal emotional growth as selfish and unnecessary, and they will, consciously and subconsciously, send that signal to the child. The child only gets recognized if it fulfills the narcissistic parent's spoken or hidden needs.

You can support your child's identity by talking about it when you are together:

- You seem to like to play a lot of sports with your friends.

- At the moment, you seem to thrive when you wake up early.

- You are very interested in history.

With these three sentences you reflect the child's interests without judging positively or negatively. If you had said, "It is very good that you like playing sports with your friends", it is judgmental – even though it is positive – and this statement is not about the child but about your experience of it.

You can do the same emotionally.

- You get sad when it feels like somebody doesn't really care for you.

- It makes you happy when others surprise you with an outdoor adventure.

- You just like sitting on the sofa and watching movies with your sister.

These are statements from you, and those words also stick in the child's memory and gives it a sense of "me" – something is the child itself and not others.

Provide the child with an opportunity to play sports or enjoy the nature with others from an early age – whether it is ballgames, the scouts, or other things close by, it will give the child a refuge and companionship with others, where it doesn't have to be on guard, and where it will learn to have sound relations with others.

If the child later says: "I don't want to do this anymore," or "Mum says that it is a stupid sport," you can say: "Okay, let's just finish this season, and then we can talk about it. It is important to finish what you start."

Children of narcissists sometimes have the same challenges as children of alcoholics. It is difficult to maintain an interest, and they find it hard to finish what they start. They need support in order to learn that.

It is typical for the narcissistic parent only to recognize activities which they themselves are interested in – everything else is stupid, useless or wrong. The child will soon take that in, and the conflict of loyalty will show again but try to support the child's interests – without discussing the other parent.

Also, the narcissistic parent will be against anything that makes the child passionate to make sure that he gets the most attention.

If the narcissistic parent confronts you with: "Why is our child a scout? That is ridiculous!" you can reply – by e-mail – something like: "We both want our child to develop sound interests in order to become an independent individual capable of solving life's challenges. I think that his/ her interest in the scouts will become a part of that development."

This is a positively manipulating formulation, and it speaks to the pride of the narcissistic parent. When the child grows older, the parent will start taking credit for the child's achievements, and therefore the parent will subconsciously find that it is a good idea to strengthen the child's development within these areas. Besides, the last sentence is only a tiny part of your own opinion; moreover, it is in the child's interest to grow into a person, whom the narcissistic parent is proud of.

As for taking credit for the child's achievements, it often happens in a child-parent-relationship with a narcissistic parent.

#EXAMPLE

Anja is a straight A-student. She is passionate about her school and about learning. Her narcissistic father only reached 7th grade, before he dropped out of school and did manual labor.

At a family event he loudly and proudly praises his daughter's performances, and her good grades, and he adds: "I took care of her as a baby and taught her everything she knows. She is truly Daddy's girl!"

The family knows about the situation, and some of them pat Anja on her back and says: "It is really great that you love learning. You can take the whole credit for your good results, and you can be very proud of that."

They don't mention the narcissistic parent, only Anja – thus taking the conflict of loyalty within Anja into consideration, and to avoid conflict with her father.

The sound parent loves the child unconditionally. Even when the parent sets boundaries and tells the child off, love lies as an unbreakable bond beneath all the words, and the child senses that.

The narcissistic parent doesn't provide that unbreakable bond of love. When the narcissistic parent scolds, it can be mean, hateful and abusive.

It can be incredibly painful to experience that your child has to go through this. However, stay focused on the child and its feelings, all the time.

Most children of narcissistic parents are not ready to break their loyalty until they are in their twenties. This happens, when the child VOLUNTARILY comes and says: "Listen. There must be something wrong with Dad!" Then you can ask: "What do you think is wrong?"

Don't let that conversation develop into being about your suppressed emotions and experiences – again, keep focus on the child or the young adult.

"I think that he is insane."

"Which experience makes you say that?" (Keep calm).

"It is like he never listens to what others say. And he doesn't respect it, when I say no. And then he talks rubbish to me and others. It isn't normal behavior!"

"I think I know what you mean. Have you heard about narcissism? Maybe your Dad carries some of those character traits. If you want to, you can read about it on the Internet, and then we can talk again?"

It is wise to avoid being the one telling your child about narcissism. Let the child read about it without your influence. In that way, you sow a seed.

During your child's upbringing, your own network is extremely important – both for you and for your child. It is important for you to have close relations, where you can get support and be open and honest.

For your child, it is important to experience healthy relations between adults, and to meet adults, who might become secondary role models – you and the other parent are the primary role models.

Secondary role models can show your child that adults are different, and that the reality can be different from the reality of the narcissist, who constantly feels that others are out to get him.

HOW DO I TALK TO THE SYSTEM?

When you talk to the system – teachers, social workers, case officers, lawyers, or other people, you might experience that they don't understand or recognize your problem.

Make sure to bring along a competent assessor for meetings; write down what they say and remain calm. When you become emotionally involved – which is natural because you are talking about your child – you can damage your own cause.

Focus on what is best for your child and remember that whenever YOU are under attack. Keep focus on the most important thing: Your child.

Keep your statements factual and avoid discussing feelings. Don't hide unsound and damaging behavior. Tell the professionals about it in neutral, short sentences without anger, sorrow, or contempt.

Perhaps you can tell the professionals that you use the Grey Rock method because your ex-partner reacts aggressively to emotional statements.

The representatives from the system might easily become flying monkeys, and therefore it is very important that you bring along an assessor for those meetings, and that you have a strong network to support you when you see the narcissist fool and charm the surroundings.

The entire experience with the system can be a frustrating and sorrowful meeting because it can be VERY difficult to explain what is happening behind closed doors at home. Therefore, you HAVE to report violence. It can cost you if you don't, even though you think that you can explain it to yourself as a "slip-up" or you feel ashamed of it happening to you. The more YOU recognize what the narcissistic parent does and has done, the better your case is when it comes to the children.

You can try to contact an organization for victims of abusive relationships. There are plenty of opportunities for getting help and support.

WHEN A CHILD IS SUBJECTED TO A NARCISSISTIC PARENT, THE CHILD DOESN'T STOP LOVING THE PARENT - IT STOPS LOVING ITSELF!

The Narcissist In The Workplace And In The System

Narcissists are everywhere – they are no longer only to be found among bosses, movie stars, or presidents. Narcissists love control, and therefore you find them in all strata of society, where they have the possibility of exercising control over people and situations.

Besides that, naturally – or sadly, there are many people, who seem narcissistic. They may not be narcissists through and through, but they have narcissistic traits. When you must interact with those people, you can handle them in a way that makes it easier for you, for example by using the Grey Rock method, which I have described in several places. Besides, you can use the following strategies:

Manipulate the narcissist by pointing out his strength. "I know that you have everything under control, and I need to talk about how we can manage our colleagues in a caring way, in order to motivate them to do their best. Have you any ideas as to how to do so?"

What you do is firstly recognize his own idea about him being skilled and knowledgeable. Secondly, you use that as a platform to point out that the communication is going to be caring – and you invite him to find a solution. Naturally, you can replace the word "caring" with another word but take care that you don't talk in general and vague terms. Using words like "appropriate" doesn't work here; the term is too wide, and it is open for interpretation – the narcissist has his own idea of what is appropriate.

Use the narcissist's own behavior to achieve what you want: "I see you as a person, who appreciates direct, open, and clear communication. We are all different people, and some of the other coworkers are not as straightforward. I think that we as managers have to provide a good working environment, and we have to use a form of communication where they feel that we notice and respect them. Perhaps we could show some consideration and an open dialogue? What would you think would be the best option?"

If the narcissist resists and says something like "they don't get it, unless we are direct," or "they just need to pull themselves together," you can say something like: "I truly understand your impatience because you talk so straightforwardly yourself. We need to respect your preference for open communication. I think that we will gain the most from our colleagues, if we respect the different ways of how to communicate. So, with you we can be direct, and with some of the others we have to be a bit more considerate. Could you agree to that?"

Generally, it might be a good idea to give the narcissist a "shit sandwich" – i.e. a critique wrapped in appraisal of something he does correctly, or of his strengths. The ideal solution would be to get rid of that person, but sometimes that is impossible, if for instance that person has been elected to a post for a certain amount of time and doesn't literally break the law.

However, you have to take care not to praise the narcissist for something he doesn't deserve appraisal for. You have to rephrase your words, and if possible, evade him if he is very abusive, for instance: "I see you as very dedicated to this cause. I think that your commitment might be used for making the coworkers feel more secure and supported, so they do their best. Do you have any suggestions as to how to accomplish that?"

Even more important than coaching the narcissist is supporting your employees into not taking other's behavior personally. That is really difficult because we are equipped with mirror neurons and read other peoples' body language, but it might be useful to offer your employees a group session or a therapy session with someone, who knows about this certain issue, and you can talk to the employees in a safe space, and who can help them practice the Grey Rock method. They must learn to let the narcissist's word bounce off like water on a goose when talking to the narcissist.

You have to create a work environment, where meetings always have at least three participants, so the narcissist never is alone with anyone – and make sure to write everything down.

For instance, you can record all meetings – openly – "to remember what was discussed" – that will probably have a positive effect on the narcissist's statements. If not, it provides you with material to build a case to get rid of the person.

It sometimes seems like the narcissist is very skilled. Or, that the narcissist truly wants the best for the company. Or even, that the person fights for the cause of the people/users/customers. It only lasts as long as the narcissist gains from it.

When the narcissist no longer gains attention from his behavior, he will become furious which can be very damaging for his surroundings/ the company/ the organization/the project. Smear campaigns, personal attacks or contacting the media – a narcissist will use any method which gives his attention.

If you are at a workplace, in an organization, or in a public office with a narcissist, you will find that he uses the strategies mentioned earlier in this book to get his own way. Gaslighting, triangulation, and lies are not uncommon. Therefore, you have to make sure that you are never alone with the narcissist.

You can also make sure that you never confide in the narcissist, and you better stay away from private functions with him. Don't let his charm fool you, but remain friendly, and stay focused on work, when you talk.

Keep away from company parties and other social functions if the narcissist is there and refrain from gossiping about the narcissist. Stay focused on the job, the cause, or the project, as much as you can. It may lessen your job satisfaction, but it will diminish further if you let the narcissist get close to you, crawl under your skin, and control you.

The narcissists' communication is often very convincing. Since they themselves think that they are right, it can be tempting to accept their beliefs or to become overwhelmed by their self-assuredness. However, often our sixth sense reacts to them, and our alarm bells sound loudly – listen to those alarm bells and take care of yourself.

Unless you find it amusing to waste your time on endless, non-constructive discussions, you must not begin an argument against them. Just listen, say that it is interesting, and make an excuse for walking away as soon as possible.

The narcissist can be quite abusive, and if you take everything he says personally, you are in danger of getting stress. When I arrange online workshops for companies, there is always at least one person, who suffers from stress and is or has been off on a sick leave. It damages the company, but it is worse for the person. Stress is a serious condition, and it is important to provide help, so stressed people learn to take better care of themselves. This also benefits the company.

#EXAMPLE

Henry is a board member in an organization. He talks a lot, and he seems to love a good debate, but he always ends up dismissing others by saying that they don't know what they are talking about. He diminishes instead of reflects.

Henry's starting point is that only he knows the truth, and if anyone tries to differentiate that picture, he becomes cross, and sometimes he walks away saying: "No one seems to really understand how serious our work here is!"

He can be very direct in his criticism toward the other board members, and he calls them ignorant and incompetent. This creates a toxic atmosphere, and it is a poor starting point for the job in hand.

The chairman and the local employee representative decide to talk to him and make him realize that his behavior is unsuitable.

The talk doesn't lead to anything. Even though they use every communicative trick in the book, Henry twists all their words around and makes it sound like they are after his head and want to get rid of him, and that is his sole focus point. He is unable to enter a discussion as to whether his behavior could become more appropriate, and he doesn't listen to or accept their examples. Instead, he claims that they lie, twist the truth, and are setting him up.

Behind Henry's back, the chairman calls for a meeting, and the board decides to put it on the agenda for the next meeting. At that meeting, they unanimously voted for his exclusion.

Henry doesn't turn up at that meeting, and he spends endless amounts of energy to write to different people to make them understand that he is being treated unfairly. The aftermath lasts almost six months, but finally the communication fades out, and the board is able to work together peacefully.

How Do You Free Yourself From A Narcissist?

WHAT YOU CAN DO FOR YOURSELF

The best you can do for yourself is to get as far away as possible and make sure to keep the distance.

Delete the narcissist's phone number, block the person on all social media, and don't pick up the phone. If some sort of contact is necessary, you can say that all messages must be sent via e-mail – and keep all your own messages short, concise, and without any show of emotions.

If you are living with the narcissist, then let your friends help you make a detailed plan for your exit – how to find another place to live, how much money you need to save, what things to bring, etc.

Keep it a secret to everyone who is not going to help you get away. People can act like flying monkeys and tell the narcissist because they think it might help you.

Don't use your children or anything else as an excuse for staying. The best thing you can do for your children and you, is to be happy, and that is the most important thing. You are not happy with the narcissist, so that is not a solution.

It is NOT the best thing for children to live with both their parents if you are unhappy. You are not a "buffer" between the narcissist and your children – they are better off, when YOU are happy and strong.

If you are afraid that the narcissist should get custody of the children, you should know that most narcissists only care for younger children.

When the children grow up, they become too hard to handle, and the narcissist will probably let you or others take care of them.

This example is about my narcissistic father, but it still gives you a clue on how to get away from a narcissistic spouse. Do not become financially dependent on a narcissist - it will be really hard to get out.

#EXAMPLE

Marianne wants to get away from Poul, with whom she has been living for 10 years. He has beaten her, and humiliated her as well as her friends and family. He has isolated her, and she has moved away from him and back again several times because he promised to improve. She knows that she has to get away, so he can't find her.

She asks her brother and a friend to help her, and for six months she saves every penny and puts them into her brother's bank account.

She finds an apartment and makes it clear for all her close friends that they under no circumstances are allowed to tell Poul about her new address or to talk about her. She knows that he will call her friends and her family and try to persuade them into telling him about her whereabouts.

She buys a new telephone with a hidden number, she sets up a camera outside her office, and she tells her colleagues about the situation and asks them to contact the police if they see him.

After six months of preparation she moves one day, when Poul is out of town, and she leaves a note saying that she has photographed all her injuries – and if he tries to find her, she will report him to the police.

Still, Poul contacts her parents and her friends, but all of them refuse to speak to him and hang up the phone. When Poul calls upon Marianne's brother, he immediately contacts the police, and Poul runs away.

Half a year later, Poul gives up and finds a new victim, and he leaves Marianne alone. When they meet five years later at a social event, Marianne simply ignores him. She doesn't say hello; she looks away when he is around, and she leaves when he walks toward her.

If the narcissist is a superior or a colleague, be sure to write down the episodes. This improves your memory if it should come to a lawsuit. Ask to bring another person to meetings, even though it is your boss. If possible, write down what happens, so everything you agreed on is in writing.

Confirm the results from the meeting by sending an e-mail to your superior stating: "I confirm that this meeting was about … "– and again: Keep it short, and don't show any emotions.

Make sure that you take care of yourself by staying in touch with your inner self, and by nurturing your mental health.

If the narcissist is a close member of your family, say it out loud that YOU don't want to have contact with this person – or send a letter, so you go no contact. If the person asks you why, you can simply say that the contact isn't good for you. Don't elaborate because the narcissist will use that to turn your own words against you, to persuade you into giving him one more chance, or to make you feel guilty, so you regret it.

Don't talk about or think about the narcissist. He wants you to use as much energy on him as possible. Move your focus. Talk about you, not him. Don't say: "Then he did this, then they said that …" etc. – but say: "I feel powerless. I feel angry. I feel abused." You can't change the narcissist by talking about the person, but you can take responsibility for your own feelings, if you talk about you – and then you can ask:

"Well, in order to make me feel better RIGHT NOW, what can I do for me?" It could be taking a long walk, watching a funny movie, reading a good book, trying out a new recipe for healthy food, getting a massage, exercising or anything else which supports and nurtures you. After all, you probably need to take care of yourself.

It sounds simple. "Is that really all?" Yes, it is exactly what you are going to do! You have to reclaim your life, make YOU the most important person in your life, find out who you are, and what it takes for you to feel good.

Every time you think about or want to talk about the narcissist, it is like drugs calling out to your inner junkie – just one more time – and you must resist it with stubbornness and perseverance.

It takes time, and you will be tempted over and over, so make sure to remind yourself about the bad things – for instance, by putting a list of them on your fridge – a fridge list.

The narcissist is your narcotics too, and it is easier to leave him, if you get help to do it. As no one can make the decision for an alcoholic to stop drinking, no one but you can decide to get away, and only you can do the hard work. You can't have a friend, or a therapist decide for you. It is YOUR decision to act upon.

THE NARCISSIST'S REACTION

You are the narcissist's drugs – and no one likes to get their narcotics taken away.

The narcissist might threaten you. Try to make friends, families, or colleagues to shame you out. Sometimes, narcissists create smear campaigns about those who want to leave them, set up boundaries, or go no contact. The purpose of those campaigns is to get your attention and make you react.

When you react, the narcissist wins.

#EXAMPLE

Jill has ended her relationship with Jake. He is furious and tries to make Jill react by sending her nasty emails about things she said and did, when they were together.

"Give me a chance to defend myself. To change. To improve. You owe me. You owe me to treat me with respect. Give me the love you promised me, but which I never got." Letters like that reach her almost daily.

Jill knows better than to react to the letters but Jake gets infuriated with her silence, and since he is unable to get a reaction from her, he sends out emails to all her contacts on social media and claims that she stole money from him, yelled at him, and hit him.

Naturally, Jill's friends are astonished, and they write to her and ask her if it is true. They suggest that Jill talks to Jake and writes that they never saw that side of her.

Jill has to spend a lot of energy explaining to them that this is Jake's strategy. He wants to hurt her through others and to make her react. Some of her acquaintances understand, others don't, and for the latter group, Jill has to put their friendship on hold for a while. The best thing for Jill in this situation is unconditional support from family and friends.

THE NARCISSIST WILL BEG YOU FOR INTIMACY AND FRIENDSHIP – AND THEN WASTE YOUR TIME.

The narcissist may also use love bombing. He may try to persuade you into coming back, if you give him the opportunity to talk to you. The narcissist uses many different strategies, but they only work if you let them. If you stay cold and don't react but keep focusing on what is good for you, the narcissist will soon turn him attention toward another victim and lose interest in you.

The narcissist will always deny or manipulate the evidence. You can never win, but if it is a person from work or a volunteer cooperation, you must make sure to document it. Bear in mind that the narcissist lies. Always. To everybody, including himself and you. Don't fall for the bluff.

A narcissist considers other people their private property, and therefore you might experience that he returns to you, if the new prey evades or fails to provide the narcissist with enough supply. He will promise you the world; tell you that he has realized his mistakes, has been in therapy, that he regrets his actions and everything else – as long as you return. Don't do it.

It has happened that narcissists make death threats toward their relatives, if they leave them – or that they threaten to commit suicide. The extremely narcissistic persons might actually do it, so don't take it lightly if he threatens you. Contact the police, talk to someone about it, and get help to handle the situation.

Only a mean and evil person will threaten to take his own life and let you take responsibility for it. You must never let a narcissist make you believe that you are responsible whether this person lives or dies. Committing suicide is the most personal thing to do in the whole world, and it has NOTHING to do with you – only with the narcissist's own feeling of emptiness.

If you have children with a narcissist who threatens to take his own life, then contact social services and tell them. Let them contact the narcissist and talk to him – it is NOT YOUR JOB because then you are trapped again.

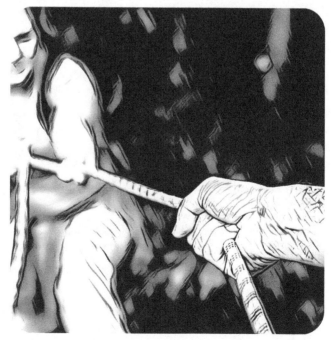

After The Narcissist

HOW DO YOU MOVE ON?

Moving on is all about you. Sometimes, when we end a relationship with another person, there is a kind of closure and evaluation. In cases with narcissists this never happens. You will never make the narcissist understand what he did to you.

You will probably never reach a point where everything suddenly makes sense. The narcissist has twisted your sense of reality so much that there will always remain some unanswered questions.

Moving on is about resetting your perception of things and about being able to put some events behind you.

After the narcissist, you are given a choice: Grow stronger, more firmly grounded, more distinct, more self-assured and less preoccupied with what others think about you – or you can repeat all the mistakes.

When you have been close to a narcissist, you might feel the need to UNDERSTAND. Why did it happen? Why did he act like that? But there is nothing to understand. The narcissist is irrational. What you can – and must – understand is YOU. Why did you choose to become a smaller person in order to survive, to feel accepted, loved, and worthy? It hurts to let yourself down time after time, to make excuses for the other person, and to cover for the person's sick behavior.

The narcissist makes you doubt whether you can manage without him. He rarely says so in the beginning, but he manipulates you into thinking that it is so, and when he finally speaks the words, he confirms the thought which he with his behavior has sewed inside your mind. But you did quite well BEFORE you met the narcissist, didn't you? If you had a good life before, it is possible to get a new, good life afterwards!

If you are the child of a narcissist, you might have experienced this as well - that your narcissistic mother has planted a story in you that you can't cope with life without him. That you will fail. Just take one step at a time in the right direction - the direction of becoming your own boss in your own life, making your own decisions, feeling what is inside you, getting to know you, accepting who you are and exploring life without fear.

IF A RELATIONSHIP HURTS YOU MORE THAN IT GIVES YOU JOY,
THEN LOVE YOURSELF ENOUGH TO LET GO.

When you have been close to a narcissistic person for a longer period, something happens to you.

Your self-worth fades, and you start doubting your own perception of the world. You feel guilt for no reason – just to mention a few of the consequences.

You need to know that even though you are out of the relationship or have severed contact with the narcissist, the consequences still reside within you.

One of the most horrible consequences is INTERPRETATION. Since you never know what the narcissist feels, what he may say, do or punish you for, you start interpreting.

That is a natural reaction, however, the narcissist is difficult to read; his behavior doesn't make sense. This means that your interpretation increases, and in the end becomes so strong that you try to make sense of other peoples' behavior too – narcissists or not. Even though you are no longer under influence from the narcissist, you will interpret other events.

#EXAMPLE

Lotte has a close friend, whom she often calls after the break-up with the narcissist. Her friend listens, and even though she is unable to completely understand what Lotte has been through, she tries to support her as much as possible. After a few months, Lotte realizes that her friend never calls her – Lotte is always the one who takes the initiative.

Immediately, Lotte's narcissism-overinterpreting-radar flares, and Lotte starts speculating why the friend never calls her. She doesn't ask her but concludes that her friend has grown tired of her. Instead of assuming that her friend is an adult woman who is able to say no, Lotte makes her one with a hidden agenda.

Lotte doesn't know her friend's agenda because that is not the way overinterpreting works – it doesn't make sense – but Lotte's intention is, subconsciously, to make herself a victim. It is common that the narcissist's relations feel victimized, even after a break-up, and their overinterpreting sends them directly into a victim mode.

Lotte calls me. She wants to enter therapy because she doesn't think that any of her friends care for her anymore. We talk. I ask if she has discussed this with any of her friends. She hasn't – and she is relieved when she realizes that she has created the drama within herself.

Lotte calls her friend and asks why Lotte always is the one to make the phone call? Her friend replies that she just wishes to be available to Lotte, and since they talk so often, she thinks it is fine that Lotte calls, when she needs it. When Lotte tells her friend about her fragile state of mind, her friend suggests that she calls Lotte every Sunday – and Lotte sheds tears of joy over her friend's thoughtfulness.

C-PTSD - TRAUMA IN THE BODY

Often, a person who has been close to a narcissist for too long will have complex post traumatic stress disorder - C-PTSD - this trauma is situated in the body, in your nervous system and must be dealt with through body work to heal. You cannot talk your way out of trauma like that. What you can do is breathing exercises, dance, therapeutic massages and yoga. Exercising does some healing, but it is not the best because it enforces tension in some parts of the body.

I have made a video with a breathing exercise for you here: https://visiblehearts.com/get-help-online-now/ and I can tell you that dancing is a strong therapeutic method. Put on some great, wild dancing music and dance around the living room wildly. Just five minutes a day will make a difference in your life. This is because music is the only thing in the world that lights up all centers of your brain, thereby creating more neural connections and it releases tension in the best way possible in the body. Shut off your brain and just let your body move to the music.

THE TEN STRATEGIES WHEN DEALING WITH NARCISSISTS AND TRAUMA

Being under the spell of a narcissist seems complicated and has complicated consequences, but the solutions are simple. First and foremost, you must start to take care of you, think of you, do good things for you and be your own best parent - no parent will accept that their child is abused and you shouldn't either.

Getting out may be as hard as giving up drugs and you might need help in holding on to what you know to be true - but you ARE the most important person in your life and you should treat you as such!

Here, we have the ten best strategies for dealing with narcissists and the after effects of being close to a narcissist.

1. Go no contact if you can or have minimal contact
2. Get everything in writing
3. Avoid meeting with the narcissist alone
4. Use the Grey Rock method - no emotional expressions
5. Do not explain or defend yourself - it is futile
6. Do not use the narcissist's own methods
7. Focus on yourself and creating a happy life
8. Work on quieting or eliminating the inner critic
9. Let go of guilt and shame
10. Dance, sing and laugh a lot

YOU ARE BRAVE BECAUSE YOU GOT AWAY. YOU ARE
SMART BECAUSE YOU SURVIVED.
YOU ARE STRONG BECAUSE YOU STAYED AWAY.
YOU ARE COOL BECAUSE YOU HELD ON TO YOURSELF.

In A New Relationship – Now What?

"If I grew up with a narcissistic parent, will I then attract narcissists?"

"If I did it once, will I then fall for a narcissist again?"

Unfortunately, yes, the risk is there.

The reason why children of narcissistic parents attract narcissistic partners is that we subconsciously get attracted to what we know – more than to what is good for us. What feels familiar and safe, even though it isn't. We know exactly how to navigate within the unsound structure – we have seen it so many times and know the drill.

It all happens in your brain. It is designed to make subconscious choices and to prefer the familiar patterns.

This was a good thing back then in our tribal culture. The tribe was only able to survive, if we stuck together through hard times and difficult conditions. If the tribe should stick together, its members had to endure and live through the unsound events.

In a way, we have "roles" to play, and we look for relationships that offer us those roles: "the unselfish helper", "the one with no boundaries", "the victim", "the disempowered" – you might even be able to name your own role.

When you are working with yourself, you have to remember two things:

- You have to become VERY good at sensing yourself.

- You need solid alternatives to the unsound behavior and way of thinking.

In the book "Your Hero's Journey - How to get rid of negative side effects from your childhood", you can find tools to help doing just those things.

EXERCISE: 4 STEPS TOWARD NEW HABITS

A good and very effective tool to change unsound behavior is "4 steps toward new habits".

1. *Find out exactly what it is you do or don't do which is unsound for you. For instance:*

   "When a person close to me seems less happy than I feel, I make myself less happy, so the other person doesn't have to feel less worthy than me."

2. *When that happens, try to locate and sense that feeling inside your stomach, just before you are going to react in the unsuitable way. Maybe you have to do it a few times in order to feel it properly. It is important that it is the feeling just BEFORE your unsuitable behavior, since that is your alarm bell which will release a new and better behavior.*

3. *Decide which behavior you wish to display instead of the unsound behavior. For instance, if you tend to make yourself smaller, you could loudly tell yourself: "I want to inspire you/the other person to become happy by being a good example of happiness. I love my joy!" – and while you say this, you breathe deeply and inhale your joy over your joy. Take your time – you have probably been rushed through your upbringing, so it is all right to insist on taking your time for you and your needs.*

4. *Practice! When we learn something new, whether it is another language, riding a bicycle, a new skill, or personal lessons, it feels awkward. To adult children of narcissists, it will often also release irritation and shame, since we have learned that we need to be perfect at everything – even before we have tried it. Be patient and know that things take time to learn – and that it is okay!*

Repeat this exercise as often as possible and do it every time you discover that you are going to react unsuitably. You can recognize that behavior as being "something which doesn't make you happy or which makes you uneasy".

I can give you encouragement:

When you grow, learn, get new insights and become better at standing by yourself, you will attract – and fall for – people who match you in your present state of mind. Every long love relationship will be better than the previous one, if you keep developing yourself.

Don't think that you have missed the opportunity for the one true love. The love keeps on growing the bigger your insight and understanding is – within you and in the rest of the world.

Remember that a narcissist falls for one who takes care of everybody else before herself/himself. It is time that you took yourself into consideration. It will prepare you for the future.

Conclusion

Thank you for being with us to the end! Thank you for having the courage to read, to gain insight, and thereby to take the first step toward reclaiming the power over your own life!

It might be a good idea to put a note in your calendar and read this book in six months' time; partly to refresh the exercises and maybe discover something which you missed the first time, and partly to find out how far you have come during the first half year.

Often, we forget to recognize our own growth – and it is extremely important to realize exactly how far we have come.

A note from Mariah Wolfe:

"We have tried to make this book as personal and relevant as possible but if you need more information about something or have an idea, you can contact me at connect@visiblehearts.com – then we will take it into consideration for our next book.

For my part, I want to tell you that I have landed safely on the other side of the consequences of my dysfunctional upbringing.

I have released myself from the shame and the horrible stories; I have become adept at setting boundaries and searching for my own happiness. I tell you this to provide you with hope. If I can do it, you can do it – find the meaning of everything; discover the joy and the peacefulness.

I have been pretty fucked up by my upbringing with a narcissistic father and an alcoholic mother – and I LOVE my life today, where I stand tall in my own light, where I am surrounded by people who support me in doing so, and who shine brightly themselves.

I am grateful for my upbringing. I would never choose it, but without it I wouldn't be where I am today – and one of the most beautiful things about being me is that I can pass on my knowledge to you; I can help to strengthen and support YOU during your process.

Making a difference to other people is one of the most beautiful things you can do."

A note from Charlotte Lindhardt:

"Not until now, after 23 years, have I dared going public and telling others about my background. The first few years after the break-up I spoke too much about the letdown and my parents. At even the smallest occasion, I confided in complete strangers in order to get some compassion and understanding.

It backfired, and I became "her with the family", Charlotte, who struggled too much with the world.

One day I decided that I had to stop being a victim. I didn't want to be defined by my family, only by me. People should like me for who I am now, not for the girl who people once felt sorry for.

What I missed the most – apart from a sound family structure – was other peoples' experiences. With this book, I am finally ready to share mine.

I am so much more than "her with the family", but she is also a part of me."

Take care of yourself – you are the most important person in your life!

Charlotte and Mariah

Review this book - to help others choose
the right book for them.

Go to Amazon:

https://www.amazon.com/dp/
B08FWRB67Z

Read more

If you want to read more about narcissism, and how you move on after traumatic experiences, I recommend these books and websites.

Wolfe, Mariah: The Power to be You.

Wolfe, Mariah and Lindhardt, Charlotte: Your Healing Journey – 9 Ways to Turn Childhood Trauma into Empowered Living.

Love, Patricia: The Emotional Incest Syndrome: What to do When a Parent's Love Rules Your Life, 2012.

There is a lot of helpful research on narcissism on the Pubmed database:

https://www.ncbi.nlm.nih.gov/pubmed/

Mariah Wolfe writes about narcissism, life, traveling and healing on her website https://www.visiblehearts.com and on Facebook:

https://www.facebook.com/BeingMariah/

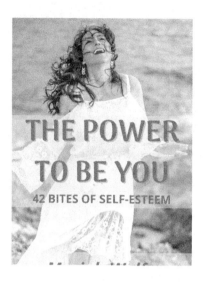

Lots of easy hands- on exercises so you can make changes right away. Through cases from Mariah's psychotherapy clinic, she illustrates and explains low self- esteem, so you can recognize yourself and find your way out.

https://www.amazon.com/dp/B087PLTWP6

You can't get rid of your childhood, but you can make it stop controlling you! Lots of examples, tools and exercises to help you get on the other side of a dysfunctional upbringing.

https://www.amazon.com/dp/B08T9Z89TS

Made in the USA
Coppell, TX
26 May 2024

32785201R00100